jewellery making
techniques book

Over 50 techniques for creating eye–catching
contemporary and traditional designs

ELIZABETH OLVER

APPLE

contents

A QUARTO BOOK

First published in the United Kingdom
by Apple Press
Sheridan House, 114 Western Road
Hove, East Sussex BN3 IDD
www. apple-press.com
Reprinted 2003, 2004, 2006

ISBN-10: 1-840923-36-9
ISBN-13: 978-1-840923-36-0

QUAR.JEMT

Conceived, designed, and produced by
Quarto Publishing plc
The Old Brewery, 6 Blundell Street
London N7 9BH

Senior Project Editor Nicolette Linton
Art Editor/Designer Sheila Volpe
Assistant Art Director Penny Cobb
Photographer Paul Forrester
Text Editors Claire Waite, Vanessa Farquharson
Indexer Pamela Ellis

Art Director Moira Clinch
Publisher Piers Spence

Manufactured by Regent Publishing Services Ltd,
Hong Kong
Printed by SNP Leefung Printers Ltd, China

Author's Acknowledgments
Miles, Beth, and Penge for their patience, help, and
support, without which this book could not have
been written.

For their expertise: Martin Baker, Graham Fuller,
John Harrison, Chris Howes, Fleur Klinkers,
Miriam Prescott, Vannetta Seecharran, Ron
Stevens, Roger Taylor, Paul Wells.

For the loan of tools, materials, and studio space:
Central Saint Martin's College of Art and Design,
EMC Services Ltd, Rashbel Ltd, Tony Jarvis Ltd,
and H.S. Walsh.

Repeated patinated steel forms undulate to entertain the eye in a necklace.

Introduction

My passion for making jewelry began in a metal workshop at school. I thoroughly enjoyed my time carving mother of pearl and soldering silver to make my first pair of earrings, little realizing at the time that I was sowing the seeds of my future.

One of the most important lessons that I learned from the skilled tutors and technicians at art school was that, beyond the ultimate need for patience, there is rarely a single definitive way of making jewelry. In fact, there are more likely to be 101 different interpretations and permutations on a theme.

The subcutaneous layer of oxidized wire creates a subtle surface pattern on this two-tone ring.

Ask three different people how they would perform the same task and you are likely to get three different answers. Don't be put off—choose the answer that most suits your way of thinking and doing, add the useful elements from the other two answers, give yourself a little time to hone your skills and gain experience, and you are likely to add a fourth solution to the equation!

A technique may have geographic and regional differences according to the expertise, tools, materials, and services that dominate the craft in that area. Even the most experienced jeweler can learn a new trick or have some small mystery explained when watching someone new tackle a familiar task.

Jewelry making is addictive because there is practically no end to the learning curve, although one need not—and indeed cannot—be a master in

Stones and other surface details are used to make patterns in these distinctive earrings.

The tactile surface of this uplifting ring conjures up delicious weather-worn treasures.

all areas since proficiency in some techniques can take many years of practice. As in all things in life, to be really good at anything you need to set your mind to the task and practice to perfect your skills.

However you choose to explore making jewelry, the important thing is to enjoy the process and the results. For some people this may be a Zen-like experience where perfection in every detail is a prerequisite; while for others it will involve the need for as near-instantaneous gratification as can be achieved with jewelry making. Whatever your approach, jewelry encompasses so many different skills and challenges there is likely to be something for everyone.

Feast your eyes on the detail in these intricate narrative brooches.

The modest bezel set stone contrasts with the fabulous proportions of this ring.

HOW TO USE THIS BOOK

Technique heading.

Example of a finished piece made using the technique.

Background information to the technique.

Equipment and materials you will need to complete the technique.

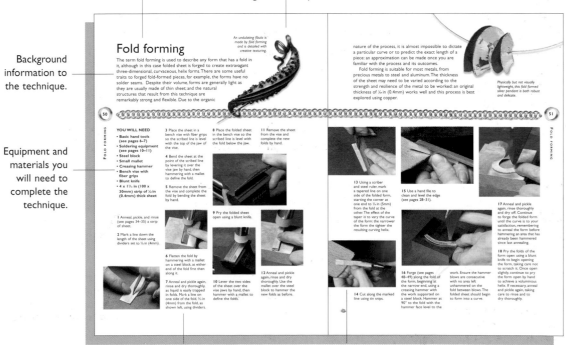

Copy explaining each stage of the technique.

Photograph showing the technique in action.

Basic hand tools

Many of the basic hand tools needed for jewelry-making have not changed in decades; some have not changed significantly in centuries. There are many tools beyond those shown here that will become useful as your skills increase and your horizons broaden; however, with a limited number of tools and skills, complex and beautiful jewelry can still be made.

To find all the tools in one place it is a good idea to visit a specialist jewelry-making tool store (see **Tools suppliers**, pages 124–125): buy metals from a bullion supplier and stones from a stone supplier (see **Bullion and stone suppliers**, pages 124–125). The cost of tools can vary a great deal according to the quality. It isn't necessary to buy top-quality tools from the outset, although it is advisable to buy the highest quality you can afford. You can build on your toolkit as your skills are expanded.

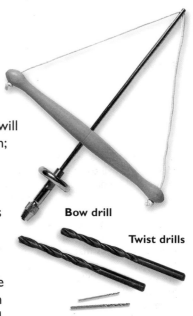

Bow drill

Twist drills

Archimedes drill

Hand drill

Bench peg and G–clamp
In the absence of a jeweler's bench (see page 10), you can start off by using a bench peg, a wooden attachment with a triangular cutout that allows for sawing, fixed to a sturdy table using a G–clamp. If you take up jewelry-making seriously then a jeweler's bench is infinitely preferable.

G–clamp

Bench peg

Saws: frames and blades
Jeweler's saw frames are either fixed or adjustable. The fixed frame is easier to tense as it is physically more flexible; the adjustable frame allows you to reuse shorter, broken saw blades. Jeweler's saw frames are much the same as those used for marquetry, dentistry, and in other trades where intricate cutting is necessary. Blades for jewelry saws are available in a variety of sizes; probably the most versatile blade is the 2/0, which is relatively fine yet robust. The finest 6/0 saw blades are used for very fine or detailed work. A general guide to choosing a blade is a minimum of 2½ teeth to the thickness of the metal.

Fixed frame

Adjustable frame and saw blades

Hand drills
Drills that can be used by hand, such as the bow drill or Archimedes drill, will be necessary if you do not have a mechanical drill such as a flexible shaft motor, also known as a pendant drill. The Archimedes, bow drill, and the traditional hand drill are limited in their usefulness as they require both hands of the maker to operate them and create the drilling action. Twist drills are the steel tool bits used in conjunction with hand drills to make holes.

Pin vise

Pin vise
A pin vise offers a means of holding small tools that are otherwise difficult to use.

Files and file handles
Jewelry files are used for removing excess material. Various grades or cuts are available for different jobs and finishes. Large jewelry files are generally used for bigger jobs, while the smaller needle files are mostly used for more intricate work. Although round, square, triangular, half-round, equaling, and warding shape make a good selection to start out with, there are many other shapes that you may eventually need (see pages 26–29). Files are available in a number of cuts from 0, the coarsest, to 6, the finest. Cut 2 is robust enough for most jobs and is a useful cut to start with. The best quality files are costly and can be damaged if stored incorrectly: files should not be placed in direct contact with other files or steel tools as these can wear the cutting surface. Mount the file in a file handle for safety and comfort.

Sanding sticks and abrasive papers

Emery sticks, emery papers, and wet-and-dry sandpaper
Jewelers traditionally used sanding papers called emery paper. Sanding sticks and papers are used for cleaning up after filing, soldering (see pages 82–83).

The longlasting and tenacious silicone carbide papers, also known as wet-and-dry sandpaper, have become increasingly popular for the same tasks. A number that refers to the number of grains to be found in a given area indicates the grade; 150 is coarse, 1200 is fine and used as a polishing paper. Though more costly than emery papers they are readily found, as they are not exclusive to the jewelry trade.

Polishing sticks, polishing compounds, and polishing threads
Felt or leather sticks are used in combination with polishing compounds for hand polishing. Store polishing tools separately from files and sanding tools to avoid contamination, and label your equipment to avoid mixing them up.

Tripoli and rouge are polishing compounds: essentially greasy compounds containing grit. Tripoli is the coarser of the two compounds and is used before rouge, which gives the fine mirror finish expected of a high polish. It is advisable to store polishing compounds separately.

Polishing threads are thin strands of cotton that can be pulled through small holes to polish fretwork.

Tripoli and rouge

Polishing stick

Polishing threads

Escapement files

Needle files

Large files

File handles

Materials

The materials most commonly associated with jewelry are silver, gold, and semiprecious and precious stones; base metals and other materials are generally useful for making rough models to test the practicality of your design. Some of the materials more recently introduced to jewelry making, such as titanium and aluminum, cannot be handled in the same way as the precious metals, primarily because they cannot be soldered. Refer to a bullion dealer for metals and stone dealer for stones (see **Bullion and stone suppliers**, pages 124–125). These are a few of the materials that you might come across when making jewelry.

Precious stones are available in a variety of cuts and shapes.

PRECIOUS METAL

Gold, silver, and platinum are traditionally described as precious metals. These are readily found in sheet, wire, rod, chenier, or as grain for casting into three-dimensional shapes. They are also fashioned commercially into tubes, chains, and fittings and findings. Some bullion dealers will also carry a variety of useful castings of settings and other commonly used forms. The cost of materials varies according to the amount of work undertaken to form it; and a surcharge called the "fashion charge" is added.

Gold

Gold can be found in numerous colors and purity, from 9 karat, as found in the United Kingdom, to 22 karat, which is used more in the Far and Middle East. In general, pure gold is too soft for jewelry purposes. Through the process of alloying, specific characteristics can be achieved such as hardness and color differences. Gold can be alloyed to make yellow, red, white, and green of various hues.

Platinum

This gray-colored inert metal is resistant to tarnishing. It is the most costly of the precious metals, partially due to its relative weight. It is good for stone setting, as it is the hardest of precious materials. Platinum needs high temperatures to solder, and casting it is a specialist job due its high melting temperature of over 2912°F (1600°C).

Platinum

Yellow gold

White gold

Silver

Semiprecious stones come in every color of the rainbow, and are opaque, translucent, or transparent.

Silver

Silver is fairly easy to handle, being a ductile and malleable metal. It is the whitest of the precious metals, although it will tarnish with exposure to air. Sterling silver (marked 925) is alloyed so that it becomes harder than fine silver, but it is less suitable than fine silver for enameling as it contains more contaminants.

PRECIOUS STONES

Precious stones are so named because of their relative rarity. They include diamonds, sapphires, emeralds, and rubies. The highest quality semiprecious stones may

actually be more costly than lower quality precious stones.

SEMIPRECIOUS STONES

The semiprecious stones are all stones other than those named as precious. They include pearls, and opaque and transparent stones. Some rare semiprecious stones can be very valuable.

BASE METALS

The term "base" refers to metals that are non-precious, including copper, gilding metal, brass, nickel, steel, aluminum, and titanium.

Copper

Copper is a ductile and malleable pinkish-red metal. It is difficult to

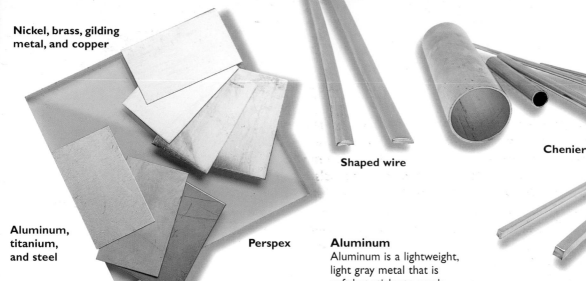

Nickel, brass, gilding metal, and copper

Shaped wire

Chenier

Aluminum, titanium, and steel

Perspex

pierce as it feels "sticky" when worked. It's a useful learning material for soldering as it is forgiving, due to its relatively high melting point of about 1904°F (1040°C)—by comparison to silver's approximate melting point of 1778°F (970°C).

Gilding metal
Gilding metal is a golden-colored metal and an alloy of copper designed for gilding. Its characteristics are similar to silver. It pierces better than copper although is slightly less malleable.

Brass
Brass is a yellow metal, harder than silver, copper, or gilding metal, although not as hard as nickel. Take care when soldering brass, as it has a relatively low melting temperature of about 1715°F (935°C).

Nickel
Nickel is a hard, pale metal with a yellowish tint that oxidizes after soldering, so needs quite a bit of cleaning up. Many people suffer from nickel allergy, so don't use it for ear posts or any other piece likely to sit next to the skin. Nickel is useful for making masters for casting (see pages 70–71) or for model-making. It is

relatively indestructible with a melting point of about 2651°F (1455°C).

Steel
Steel is a gray-colored metal known for its hardness. It is often used for tool-making. Steel comes in a variety of forms including stainless, which avoids the characteristic problem of rusting. Steel oxidizes easily so soldering can be challenging. It needs a different pickle to the precious and base metals already mentioned.

Titanium
Titanium is a hard, light, refractory metal that appears gray. It can be colored through anodizing or by heating, although there is little control when using heat. It isn't possible to solder titanium, so it makes a useful soldering aid as it has a high melting temperature. Titanium is harder than steel and can damage tools such as files and rolling mills.

Aluminum
Aluminum is a lightweight, light gray metal that is soft but sticky to work. It can't be soldered and is a contaminant, so use separate tools.

OTHER MATERIALS
Practically anything can be used for jewelry— from glass and pebbles to "found" objects such as bottle tops and feathers. Each material should be considered for its merits and treated, taking into account its vulnerabilities and durability.

Perspex
Perspex is a good quality hard plastic that comes in a variety of forms. Made from solid sheets and rods, it comes in many different colors, and can be opaque, translucent, or transparent. Perspex can be formed to a certain extent by applying heat, so it is malleable; when cooled it will set into its new form.

Resins
Resins are liquid plastics used for pouring, and so can be cast or embedded. Polyester embedding resin is difficult to handle and

produces unpleasant fumes, so avoid this type. Two-part epoxy resin is a little more costly but is easier to handle and dries tack free.

Wood
Wood is often seen in jewelry as it is relatively easy to carve and adds warmth and color. Always wear a facemask when cutting and sanding wood, to avoid breathing in dust as this can be harmful. Seal, protect, and enhance wood with wax.

Leather and fabric
Leather and fabric are popular for jewelry, as they add color and texture. Consider future cleaning and repair when planning your design. Framing will hide edges that may fray, and will protect the material from body oils.

Fixtures and findings

Measurements and weights:

General data and conversion tables

It is helpful to know certain basic data about materials when considering your options; relative weight can affect function and cost while the melting temperatures may affect your planning of a soldering job. Although the metric system of measurement is commonly used, some people still feel more at home with imperial measures, while others use both forms of measurement in conjunction.

Wire is available in a variety of gauges, so is suitable for knitting or forging.

Composition, melting point, and specific gravity of common metals

Metal	Composition (% of main element/s)	Melting point °F (°C) (approx.)	Specific gravity
Aluminum	100% A	1220 (660)	2.7
Brass	67% Cu, 33% Zn	1715 (935)	8.4
Bronze	90% Cu, 10% Zn	1922 (1050)	8.8
Copper	100% Cu	1981 (1083)	8.9
Gold 24Y	100% Au	1945 (1063)	19.3
Gold 22Y	91.6% Au	1796 (980)	17.7
Gold 18Y	75% Au	1760 (960)	15.5
Gold 14Y	58.5% Au	1598 (870)	13.4
Gold 9Y	37.5% Au	1652 (900)	11.2
Iron	100% Fe	2795 (1535)	7.9
Lead	100% Pb	621 (327)	8.9
Nickel	100% Ni	2651 (1455)	1.4
Silver (fine)	100% Ag	1762 (961)	10.6
Silver (sterling)	92.5% Ag	1688 (920)	10.4
Platinum (fine)	100% Pt	3225 (1774)	21.4
Platinum	95% Pt	3173 (1745)	20.0
Steel (ordinary)	99% Fe	2606 (1430)	7.8
Steel (stainless)	90% Fe	2642 (1450)	7.8
Titanium	100% Ti	3272 (1800)	4.5

Brown and Sharpe gauge to millimeters

Brown and Sharpe is an old-fashioned imperial form of measurements that you may come across.

B and S	mm
4	5.2
6	4.1
8	3.3
10	2.6
12	2.1
14	1.6
16	1.3
18	1.0
20	0.8
22	0.60
24	0.50
26	0.40
28	0.30
30	0.25
32	0.20
34	0.15
36	0.13
38	0.10

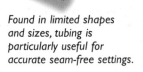

Found in limited shapes and sizes, tubing is particularly useful for accurate seam-free settings.

Separate and store your stones in types to limit damage.

Gem Stone Hardness

Using Mohs' scale of hardness —10 is hardest, 1 is softest

Stone	Mohs' scale
Amber	2–2.5
Amethyst	7
Andalusite	7–7.5
Aquamarine	7.5–8
Coral	3.5
Diamond	10
Emerald	7.5–8
Garnet	6.5-7.5
Iolite	7–7.5
Jadeite	6.5–7
Jet	3.5
Lapis lazuli	5.5
Malachite	3.5
Moonstone	6–6.5
Opal	5–6.5
Pearl	2.5–3.5
Peridot	6.5–7
Ruby/sapphire	9
Spinel	8
Tanzanite	6
Topaz	8
Tourmaline	7–7.5
Turquoise	6
Zircon	6.5

Inch fractions to millimeters

inch	mm	inch	mm	inch	mm
1/16	1.6	1 1/16	27.0	2 1/16	52.4
1/8	3.2	1 1/8	28.6	2 1/8	54.0
3/16	4.8	1 3/16	30.2	2 3/16	55.6
1/4	6.4	1 1/4	31.8	2 1/4	57.2
5/16	7.9	1 5/16	33.3	2 5/16	58.7
3/8	9.5	1 3/8	34.9	2-3/8	60.3
7/16	11.1	1 7/16	36.5	2 7/16	61.0
1/2	12.7	1 1/2	38.1	2 1/2	63.5
9/16	14.3	1 9/16	39.7	2 9/16	65.1
5/8	15.9	1 5/8	41.3	2 5/8	66.7
11/16	17.5	1 11/16	42.9	2 11/16	68.3
3/4	19.1	1 3/4	44.5	2 3/4	69.9
13/16	20.6	1 13/16	46.0	2 13/16	71.4
7/8	22.2	1 7/8	47.6	2 7/8	73.0
15/16	23.8	1 15/16	49.2	2 15/16	74.6
1	25.4	2	50.8	3	76.2

Cutting list

When planning a project you will need to make a list of the metals you need, with dimensions, for the process of placing an order. This list is commonly known as a cutting list. If you are ordering precious metal it may be necessary to know the weight of the material to consider if you can afford to proceed without alterations to your design or choice of materials.

Useful information regarding weight

The ounce used to weigh precious metals is known as a troy weight. There are 12 troy ounces to the pound. One troy ounce is approximately equal to 31 grams. The troy ounce is about 10% heavier than the avoirdupois ounce.

Base metals are weighed using the avoirdupois system. There are 16 avoirdupois ounces to the pound. One avoirdupois ounce is roughly equal to 28 grams. The avoirdupois pound is about 21.5% heavier than the troy pound.

Formulae for calculations: computing the weight of sheet, wire, and shot

Weights in grams (g), measurements in millimeters (mm)

Rectangular or square sheet: Length x width x thickness x specific gravity ÷ 1,000 = gram weight

For example, the weight of a piece of 18 carat gold sheet that is 60mm in length, 5mm in width, and 2mm in depth is calculated:

60 x 5 x 2 x 15.5 ÷ 1,000 = 9.3g

Rectangular or square wire: Wire thickness x wire depth x length x specific gravity ÷ 1,000 = gram weight

For example, the weight of a length of square sterling silver wire 4mm square, 200mm in length is calculated:

4 x 4 x 200 x 10.4 ÷ 1,000 = 33.28g

Round wire: This is calculated in the same way as rectangular or square wire, although the calculation must find the circumference of the wire.

1/2 of the diameter, squared, x 3.14 x length x specific gravity ÷ 1,000 = gram weight

For example, the weight of a length of platinum round wire 3mm in diameter, 55mm in length is calculated:

1.5^2 x 3.14 x 55 x 21.4 ÷ 1,000 = 8.32g

Round piece of sheet: 1.2 of the diameter, squared, x 3.14 x thickness x specific gravity ÷ 1,000 = gram weight

For example, the weight of a disc of fine silver 300mm in diameter, 1.5mm in thickness is calculated:

150^2 x 3.14 x 1.5 x 10.6 ÷ 1,000 = 1123.34g

Solid spherical object: 1/2 of the diameter, cubed, x 4.189 x specific gravity ÷ 1,000 = gram weight

For example, the weight of a piece of steel shot 10mm in diameter is calculated:

5^3 x 4.189 x 7.8 ÷ 1,000 = 32.67g

jewelry making techniques

Whileile studying jewelry at the Royal College of Art in London, I was fortunate enough to meet some of the leading lights in the field of jewelry. These jewelers were all artists, practitioners, and specialists. No matter where they came from—the United States of America, Australia, Holland, Israel, Japan, or the United Kingdom—they were all exemplary because they had achieved the highest standards in jewelry. And the single most striking impression I gained from watching these jewelers working at the bench was the sense of enjoyment they had for their subject.

Enjoyment is a very important factor in jewelry making, as is quality, and whether it is the simplest piece or the most intricate creation, it takes time, practice, patience, and passion to achieve really good quality results, so you must enjoy the process.

It is hard to reach the zenith in one branch of the discipline, let alone hope to reach such heights across the board. Try as many techniques as you can, then choose those that really excite you to act as the fuel for your passion.

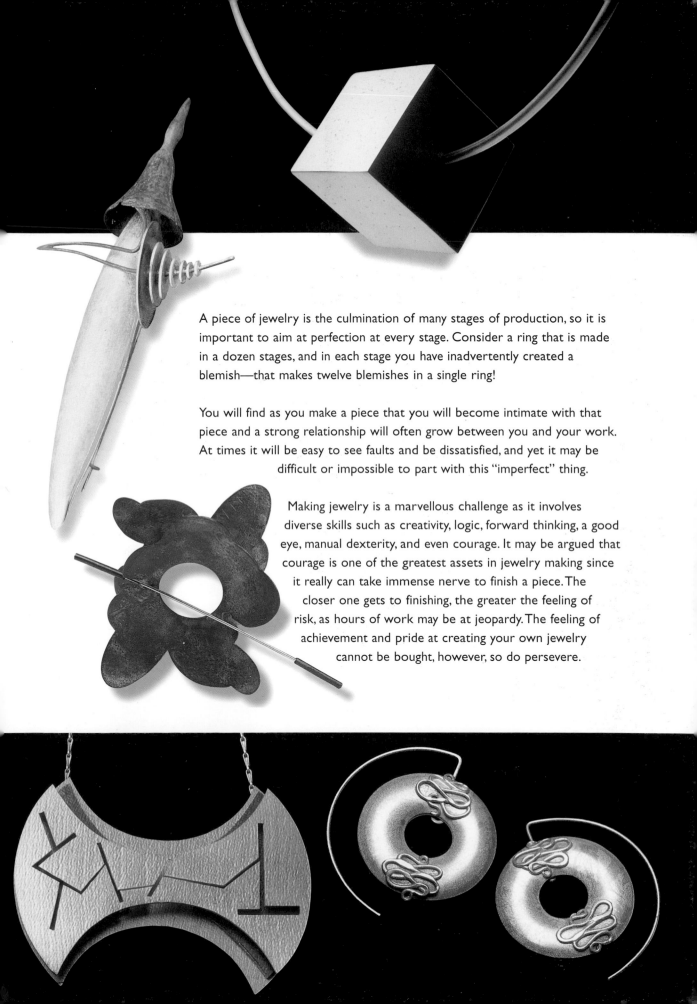

A piece of jewelry is the culmination of many stages of production, so it is important to aim at perfection at every stage. Consider a ring that is made in a dozen stages, and in each stage you have inadvertently created a blemish—that makes twelve blemishes in a single ring!

You will find as you make a piece that you will become intimate with that piece and a strong relationship will often grow between you and your work. At times it will be easy to see faults and be dissatisfied, and yet it may be difficult or impossible to part with this "imperfect" thing.

Making jewelry is a marvellous challenge as it involves diverse skills such as creativity, logic, forward thinking, a good eye, manual dexterity, and even courage. It may be argued that courage is one of the greatest assets in jewelry making since it really can take immense nerve to finish a piece. The closer one gets to finishing, the greater the feeling of risk, as hours of work may be at jeopardy. The feeling of achievement and pride at creating your own jewelry cannot be bought, however, so do persevere.

Piercing

Whether used for complex decorative fretwork or for basic shape cutting, piercing needs to be mastered for accuracy and efficiency.

The tension of the saw blade is of paramount importance: if a blade is not set properly it will wander, which makes piercing with accuracy almost impossible. To ensure that a pierced image in sheet is the same front and back, the saw blade must be used vertically. If the blade is used at an angle, it is

Simple, round earrings are made three dimensional with a split, a tweak, and a little detailing.

Preparing to pierce

YOU WILL NEED

- **Basic hand tools, including piercing saw and 2/0 saw blades (see pages 6–7)**
- **2⅜ x 1⁹⁄₁₆ in (60 x 40mm) strip of ¹⁄₃₂ in (0.8mm) thick sheet**
- **Oil or wax**

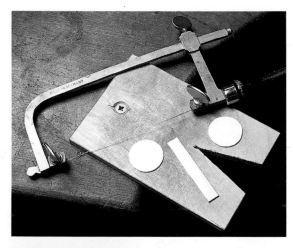

An adjustable saw frame lets you use different lengths of blade and so allows you to carry on using a broken blade, if it is not too short.

A fixed saw frame is easier to tense and more flexible than an adjustable frame.

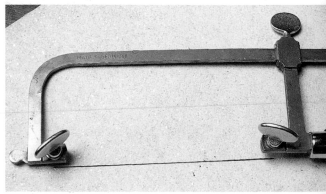

You need to set an adjustable saw frame to the correct length for the length of blade being used.

also more difficult to turn the saw blade to change direction; a vertical saw blade turns by cutting a tiny column-shaped hole, while an angled saw blade cuts a cone-shaped hole.

Saw blades are available in a variety of sizes, from 4—the heaviest—through 0 to 0/6—the finest—which you may choose for particularly detailed fretwork or when working with very thin sheet (see **Saws: frames and blades**, page 6).

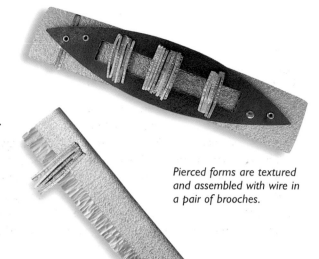

Pierced forms are textured and assembled with wire in a pair of brooches.

1 Hold a saw blade against the saw frame with the teeth pointing down to the handle and outward from the frame.

2 Place the blade in the bottom knuckle and tighten the nut firmly.

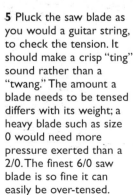

3 Prepare to tense the blade. Sit at the bench and rest the top of the saw frame against the bench peg. Cup the handle of the frame in your secondary hand (your left hand if you are right-handed and vice versa), so that you can push against the bench peg.

4 Lean your body weight on the handle of the saw frame so that the top of the blade is forced upward to the top of the frame. Hold that position, drop the saw blade into the top knuckle, then tighten the knuckle so that it holds the blade in a state of tension.

5 Pluck the saw blade as you would a guitar string, to check the tension. It should make a crisp "ting" sound rather than a "twang." The amount a blade needs to be tensed differs with its weight; a heavy blade such as size 0 would need more pressure exerted than a 2/0. The finest 6/0 saw blade is so fine it can easily be over-tensed.

6 To check that the saw blade is correctly loaded, run your finger up the blade as it faces out of the saw frame. Your finger should "catch" against the teeth. If your finger runs smoothly up the saw blade, it is loaded incorrectly; it may be upside down, facing back into the frame, or both. If it is not loaded correctly take the blade out and start again from step 1.

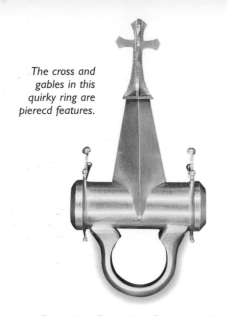

The cross and gables in this quirky ring are pierced features.

Wax or oil can be used as a lubricant to keep the saw blade running smoothly as both blade and material get hot and "dry" while cutting, causing the blade to break more easily.

Piercing is an essential skill that cannot easily be replaced with mechanical cutting, especially as the scale of the work may be small and forms are often three-dimensional and irregular, making setting up for mechanical cutting impractical. At times, the depth of a line to be cut may exceed the depth of the piercing saw

PIERCING

Piercing a straight line and a circle

There will be many instances where accurate piercing of a straight line will be required, so it is a good idea to try a few practice runs to get you used to this skill. A circle is the most telling curve, since if it is not true the eye can easily detect inaccuracy.

7 To mark out the strip of metal sheet for piercing, set a pair of dividers to ⅜ in (10mm).

8 Hold one arm of the dividers against the long edge of the metal strip and draw the other arm down to scribe a straight line, parallel ⅜ in (10mm) from the edge.

9 Use the dividers to divide the remaining strip into two squares.

10 Use the dividers to mark the center of the two squares and scribe two 1 in (25mm) diameter circles.

11 Place the sheet on the bench peg so that the line to be cut is over the "V" shaped cutout, but with as much of the sheet as possible braced on the peg. A jeweler's bench usually has a single fixed bench peg with a "V"-shaped cutout for piercing, however, a separate peg that allows the work to be turned and kept horizontal can also be attached. If you are right-handed it should be attached on the left-hand side of the cutout in the bench, and vice versa. Attach the piercing peg with a single countersunk screw centered 1 in (25mm) from the top edge so that it is firmly held, but not so firmly that it cannot turn. A fixed peg can be turned so that the slanted face is used for filing and the flat face for piercing.

frame, so if you want to pierce long lines or larger forms, you would need to use a deep throated piercing saw. These come in a variety of sizes and are not as easy to handle as a standard piercing saw. This is because the physical balance of the deep throated saw is altered by the extended frame, making it more difficult to control.

Special saw blades are used for cutting wax and Perspex, where the material is inclined to reseal itself as it is pierced due to the heat that is being generated by the cutting action.

Pierced discs are formed to make a hollow pendant detail for a conceptual ring.

PIERCING

12 Hold the sheet with your secondary hand, with your fingers positioned close to the line to be cut. Grip the saw handle lightly in your primary hand so that you can flex your wrist easily to ensure the blade is used vertically.

13 Aim to cut next to the line you have marked rather than on it, so that when you have finished piercing you still have your marked line as a reference for filing (see page 28). To start the cut, run the blade upward on the edge of the sheet at the proposed point of entry.

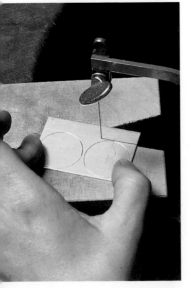

14 Using very little forward force, move the saw up and down using the full length of the blade, keeping a steady rhythm. Continue cutting until you reach the end of the marked line, concentrating on keeping the blade vertical.

15 To pierce a circle you need to cut into the sheet from the edge until you are just outside the scribed line, again leaving the line visible for filing.

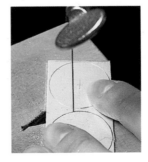

16 You will need to change direction to begin cutting the circle. Without using forward pressure, keep the saw moving up and down on the spot, in a steady rhythm, taking care to keep the blade vertical. Using your secondary hand, turn the sheet by degrees until the blade runs freely. Remember that the blade has a width a tiny bit smaller than its depth, so the amount that it needs to cut to change direction is tiny, and if your blade is vertical a change of direction is quick and the hole made small and neat.

17 Continue cutting the sheet with your secondary hand, turning to pierce the whole circle. Look to where you want to end up to achieve a smooth, flowing line, By forcing the piercing saw into a different direction you will end up with a noticeable change of direction.

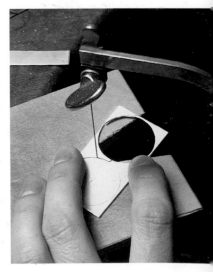

18 Repeat steps 15 to 18 to cut the second circle.

Fretwork

Fretwork is the term used to describe perforations in sheet metal that form a pattern of positive and negative shapes. Holes are drilled into the metal to pass a saw blade though, so a negative shape can be cut. There is no simple alternative to piercing, nor is there a simple mechanized method that will do the job as well as piercing, so it is essential to spend time perfecting this skill.

Fretwork takes practice. Be aware that the blade is most easily broken on changes of direction. Thick sheet is more problematic than

Engraving is used to add further sumptuous detail to a fretwork silver dragon.

YOU WILL NEED

- **Basic hand tools, including piercing saw and 2/0 saw blade (see pages 6–7)**
- **Hand or pendant drill and $^1/_{32}$ in (1mm) diameter twist drill bit**
- **Photocopied cipher or pattern**
- **Pen**
- **Double-sided adhesive tape**
- **Scissors**
- **1$^9/_{16}$ in (40mm) square, according to your cipher size, of $^1/_{16}$ in (2mm) thick sheet**
- **White spirit**
- **Soft cloth**

1 To check that the pattern is suitable for fretwork, color in the negative spaces on a photocopy and see if the positive spaces are still held in position: for example, to cut an "O" you need a tab between the center of the "O" and the rest of the sheet or you will end up with a hole instead of an "O."

2 Photocopy the pattern so that you can keep the original to refer to, adjusting the size on the copier if required.

3 Completely cover the back of the pattern with double-sided adhesive tape, without overlapping the tape and causing raised areas.

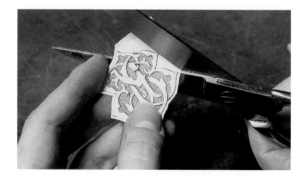

4 Trim around the pattern leaving a $^1/_{16}$ in (2mm) border.

5 Remove the tape backing from the paper and stick the pattern close to the edges on the metal sheet, so you don't have far to cut when piercing begins, and to avoid unnecessary waste.

6 Drill a number of access holes (see page 32) inside the shapes to be cut (the shaded areas), about $^1/_{32}$ in (1mm) away from the pattern (the unshaded areas). Position the holes where a line changes direction, such as a corner or the tip of a shape. Avoid positioning a hole halfway along a long, smooth line as you will see clearly the point on the line where you start and finish cutting.

thin, for example. If you do not keep your blade vertical, the pattern will be noticeably different between the top and bottom faces, a discrepancy that will not be as obvious in thin sheet. Turning is also more difficult in thicker sheet if you do not keep your saw blade vertical.

By piercing a fretwork cipher or intricate pattern in relatively thick sheet you can practice turning and piercing a variety of shapes and lines. There are a variety of free patterns suitable for fretwork in specialist "out-of-copyright" books featuring designs and images that can be reused.

Fretwork is used to add subtle detail to a gold and lapis lazuli ring.

FRETWORK

7 Load the saw blade into the bottom knuckle of the saw frame, then pass the saw blade through a hole so the pattern is facing upward in the saw frame.

8 Let the sheet drop to the bottom of the knuckle so that you don't need to support the work. Tense the blade.

9 Pierce the pattern (see pages 24–25). If you are right-handed, cut in a clockwise direction, so that the pattern is to the right of the saw blade and the line is not obscured by it. If left-handed, cut counterclockwise.

10 If you break a blade, drill another hole nearby rather than passing your blade along the line you have already cut. If your blade becomes stuck, raise the work off the bench peg and let go of the sheet. It will spring into a position where there is no resistance on the saw blade. Reposition the work flat on the peg, hold the saw frame at the new angle, and continue cutting until the shape drops out.

11 Repeat steps 7–9 until you have cut out all the negative shapes.

12 Cut out the exterior shape. To avoid obscuring the pattern with the blade, cut counterclockwise if you are right-handed and clockwise if left-handed.

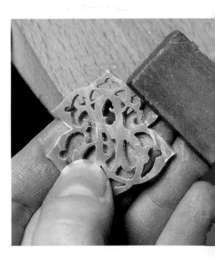

13 Peel off the photocopied pattern. Remove residual stickiness with white spirit on a soft cloth in a well-ventilated area, away from naked flames. Sand away any residue using a sanding stick (see pages 82–83).

Filing

Filing removes material by pushing a cutting face over the surface of the metal. It is used to define forms cut by piercing, for thinning the metal wall for a bezel stone setting, to thin or sharpen wire for brooch pins, or to add "shadowing" or low relief on sheet. Files are available in a variety of shapes, sizes, and cuts. The shape of file you choose depends on the job for which it is required. Flat-faced files are used to file straight edges or convex curves, while curved files are used on concave curves. The cut relates to the

A square pendant is filed and sanded to produce crisp lines and perfect form.

Filing straight lines

YOU WILL NEED

- **Basic hand tools (see pages 6–7)**
- **Strip of sheet**
- **Circle of sheet**
- **Wide rectangular section and round section ring**
- **Fretwork strip**

1 To file a straight edge you need to use a flat-faced file. Hold a strip of metal sheet firmly against the bench peg. Place the flat face of the file on the straight edge to be filed. With a downward force, push the file forward, taking care to keep the file level so that you do not file a bevel.

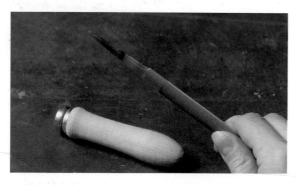

2 At the end of the stroke lift the file off the work. Do not slide the file back to the start position, this is bad practice and inaccurate, since the seesaw action causes a dip at either end of a straight edge.

3 Check the surface and changes in its reflection as it is affected by filing. Decide how to place your file for the next filing action to correct or continue a file mark. It is helpful to have a line marked on your work as a guideline for filing. Check progress against guidelines to establish where you need to file more or less.

SPECIALIST FILES
Escapement files
Escapement files are tiny specialist files commonly used by watchmakers.
Riffler files
Specialist curved files, called riffler files, are available for filing inaccessible straight or curved areas.

Files should be used with a handle for comfort and safety. To fit a wooden handle, hold the file near the top and heat about 1 in (25mm) of the tang with a soldering torch until it is red hot. Push the file firmly into the wooden handle and repeat until it is firmly in place.

amount of material a file will remove and the surface finish it will leave. A relatively coarse cut, a cut 0, is used for the quick removal of material, and will leave a heavily scratched surface. Cut 2 is a good general-purpose cut, it also removes material quickly, and the scratches it leaves are easily removed by sanding. Cuts 4, 5, and 6, also known as polishing files, leave very fine scratches. Specialist Valtitan files can be bought for filing titanium; titanium is harder than steel and thus it will damage ordinary files.

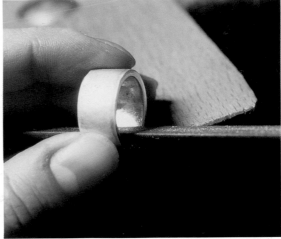

The curves of these hollow earrings are filed to remove any blemishes.

Filing convex curves

1 Use a flat-faced file to file a convex curve. Hold the disk firmly against the bench peg. Place the flat face of the file on the edge of the disk, and, with a downward force, push the file forward with care. Use a sweeping action with the file so that it follows the curve of the line, and concentrate on keeping the file level.

2 Lift the file off the work at the end of each stroke.

3 Check the surface and changes in its reflection as it is affected by filing. Decide how to place your file for the next filing action to correct or continue a file mark. As with filing a straight line, check progress against the guideline.

Filing concave curves

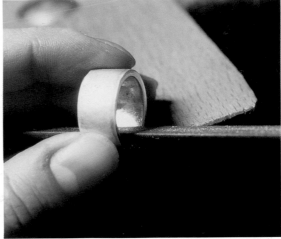

1 To file a concave edge, use a curved file. The half-round file can be too wide to fit into some ring forms, so a narrower file, called a ring file, is used. Hold the ring firmly against the bench peg. Place the curved face of the file inside the ring shank and with a downward force, push the file forward with care, using a sweeping action that follows the curve.

2 Lift the file off the work at the end of each stroke; as with a straight edge, sliding the file back to the start position can cause thinning at the edges of the ring shank.

3 Check the reflection (see step 3, **Filing convex curves**, left).

4 Turn the ring around so that you file from both sides.

Skilled and accurate filing contribute to the precision of this bold ring.

Files will "clog" with use as material is left in the cutting grooves. An easy way to clean a file is to push a metal sheet or copper coin in a diagonal direction across the face—the metal or coin acts as a comb and removes excess material from the grooves.

Filing looks simple, however, it takes practice and concentration to file with accuracy. The best indicator for accuracy is the metal's surface reflection that is produced by the filing process: if the reflection is curved you will know that your line is not straight.

Filing ring shanks

1 To file the outside of a wide ring shank, use a flat-faced file. Hold the ring firmly against the bench peg or in your secondary hand. Place the flat face of the file against the surface to be filed. With a downward force, push the file forward with care, keeping the file face flat against the flat face of the ring to avoid thinning the edge.

2 Lift the file off the work at the end of each stroke. Sliding the file back to the start position will also cause thinning at the edge.

3 To file inside a round-section ring use a curved file, either a half-round or a ring file (see **Filing concave curves**, page 29). Hold the ring firmly against the bench peg. Place the curved face of the file inside the ring shank and with a downward force, push the file forward with care, using a sweeping action

that follows the curve. You will need to adjust the angle of the file in line with the curvature of the edge of the ring.

4 Lift the file off the work at the end of each stroke.

5 To file the outside of the ring use a flat-faced file. Hold the ring firmly against the bench peg or in your secondary hand. Place the flat face of the file on the surface to be filed, and, with a downward force, push the file forward with care. Use a sweeping action with the file that follows the curve of the line, and concentrate on keeping the file level. Change the angle of the file to account for the curvature of the ring shank.

6 Lift the file off the work at the end of each stroke.

Files used on materials such as aluminum or lead will be contaminated, as material will be left in the fine grooves of the file face and can be deposited into fine metal. Keep a well-marked selection of files for the purpose. Files can be used to work wax, although if they are not cleared frequently they will clog. Remove the wax by warming the file gently with a flame and use a tissue to soak away the melted wax.

Filing is used to finish the fretwork and achieve the perfect fit for the hinge of this locket.

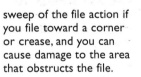

Filing fretwork

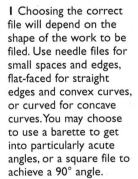

1 Choosing the correct file will depend on the shape of the work to be filed. Use needle files for small spaces and edges, flat-faced for straight edges and convex curves, or curved for concave curves. You may choose to use a barette to get into particularly acute angles, or a square file to achieve a 90° angle.

2 Follow the instructions for **Filing straight lines**, **Filing convex curves**, or **Filing concave curves** (see pages 28–29) depending on the area of fretwork being filed.

3 To file a crease or corner detail, place the file edge into the crease or corner and file away from it. You will not be able to complete the full sweep of the file action if you file toward a corner or crease, and you can cause damage to the area that obstructs the file.

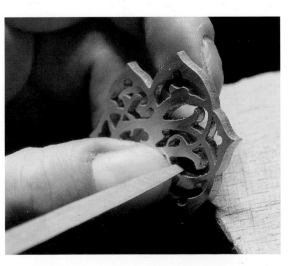

4 Filing internal spaces is difficult, as there is little room for the natural sweep of the file action. An escapement file would be necessary for extra fine fretwork.

Drilling

Drilling holes for fretwork allows a saw blade to be passed through the metal sheet to access a predefined shape for cutting. Larger holes should be started with a small drill, and worked upward to the size required. Drilling is also used for riveting, so that tube or wire can be passed though a number of sheets or pieces of metal. Holes may also be needed for other decorative reasons: to attach pendants with jump rings, to allow a piece to be hung, or when using

Holes are drilled for rivets and piercing in these layered earrings.

YOU WILL NEED

- **Basic hand tools (see pages 6–7)**
- **Archimedes, bow, or pendant drill and ¹⁄₃₂ in (1mm) diameter twist drill bit**
- **Prepared paper pattern attached to sheet (see Fretwork, pages 26–27)**
- **Wide ring**
- **Pen**
- **Oil or wax**

1 Load a twist drill bit according to the instructions for your drill, ensuring that it is held securely.

2 Mark a point on your pattern inside a shape to be cut, about ¹⁄₃₂ in (1mm) away from the pattern if possible. Mark points on all the areas to be cut.

TIP
A twist drill bit is relatively vulnerable and, if possible, should be loaded so that as much of the shank—the smooth area of the drill bit—is held by the chuck as is possible, without covering the spiral section. When drilling, always hold the work firmly against a solid wood surface. Make sure the work is held level if drilling with a bow or Archimedes drill.

3 The tip of a twist drill bit is pointed, so when presented to a metal sheet it can slip. Make an indentation on each pen mark by pushing the tip of a scriber down hard into the sheet to crease an indent on the point marked.

taps and dies to make nuts for a screw fitting.

Drilling a large number of holes by hand can be tedious. A pendant drill is a motorized unit that can be used for drilling. Always wear safety glasses when using a mechanical drill. When drilling large holes, begin with a small hole, then enlarge it by using a slightly larger drill bit each time.

Stone set pendants are attached through holes drilled in the shank of one of a pair of rings.

Layers of detail are attached to the main form through a series of drilled holes.

4 The friction caused by drilling heats up and dries the drill bit and metal sheet. Apply oil or wax to the drill bit to lubricate it. Lubrication helps to avoid the drill bit getting stuck or breaking—if the drill bit gets stuck while drilling, the piece can spin out of your grip, which is both alarming and dangerous.

5 When using a hand drill, hold the work firmly on a bench or level bench peg. Position the end of the drill bit in the indentation. Hold the work with one hand while you operate the drill with the other by raising and lowering the movable nut on the Archimedes drill.

6 When using a pendant drill, hold the work firmly against the bench. Position the end of the drill bit in the indentation. Using firm, but not hard, pressure, push the twist drill bit downward to drill the hole. Do not force the drill, which can result in the twist bit breaking. Present the drill bit so that you drill a little at a time, rather than as a single action.

Annealing and pickling

Metal hardens as it is worked or manipulated by processes such as hammering, stretching, twisting, folding, and bending. The more the metal is worked the harder it will become. Metal is heated to a specific temperature to soften it, in a process called

Metal is annealed before forming the pendant and bail in this lavish neckpiece.

YOU WILL NEED

- **Basic hand tools** (see pages 6–7)
- **Soldering equipment** (see pages 10–11)
- **Metal, sheet or 10/11 wire**
- **Silver polishing cloth**

1 Use a soldering mat on the bench to protect it from heat. Prop the metal to be annealed up against a soldering block, or on steel mesh so that heat can circulate easily around it. A turntable, with a soldering block and/or mesh, allows you to rotate the work as you heat it.

3 Annealing temperatures differ from one metal to another. As a general rule for gold, silver, copper, gilding metal, nickel, and brass, the metal is annealed when it glows a dull cherry red. Stop heating at this point. Platinum is annealed when it reaches white heat. Since the color of the metal is used as a gauge for when it is annealed, avoid heating under strong lighting or in direct sunlight, where it is difficult to see color changes.

Understanding the flame from a soldering torch will help with heating. The hottest point on the flame is at the tip of the inner of the two blue flames, about two-thirds down the length of the whole flame.

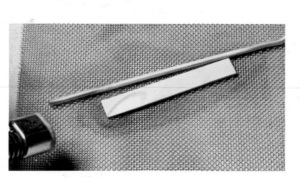

2 Anneal the metal by heating it with a soldering torch. Hold the torch in your secondary hand so your primary hand is free to use other tools. Choose the flame size according to the size of the piece being heated. Avoid using too small a flame. Metal can be heated quickly until it reaches the right temperature (see step 3), then moderate the flame to make sure you don't overheat it.

annealing. The metal is then either air cooled or quenched in water before it is pickled, a process that uses a chemical solution to remove the black oxide layer that results from heating. Platinum and pure gold do not oxidize because they are inert metals. The most common pickle for non-ferrous metals is made up of one part sulfuric acid to nine parts water. Specialist commercial solutions can be bought for pickling ferrous metals.

Sheet must be annealed as part of the pressing process for this pendant.

4 Let the metal air-cool for a few seconds. Hold the slightly cooled metal in a pair of tweezers and plunge into a container of water.

In this silver ring, metal will be annealed before it is swaged and formed into a tube.

6 Always use safety glasses and gloves when pickling. Use pickle tongs to place the work in the pickle solution. Leave the work submersed in the solution until the surface is free of oxide, and remove with the tongs. Pickling is quickened with heat; use a small Pyrex dish over a nightlight or an electric slow cooker with ceramic dish and lid .

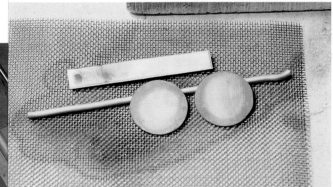

5 The pickle solutions used to remove oxide from the metals in step 3 are alum (known as safety pickle, alum is mixed with water as per the manufacturer's instructions); or a dilute sulphuric acid solution, one part sulphuric acid to nine parts water (always add acid to cold water when mixing). Do not put steel—such as binding wire—into pickle, as it causes a reaction resulting in copper plating. Steel requires specialist commercial pickling solutions.

7 Rinse the pickled metal well under running water. The dull surface bloom left after pickling can be removed by buffing with a silver polishing cloth.

Roll milling sheet and wire

The rolling mill is a simple device—similar to a mangle, used for squeezing the water from laundry. Rolling mills for metal have steel rollers, instead of rubber ones, so that they can compress metal as it is passed between them. Some rolling mills have indents for rolling

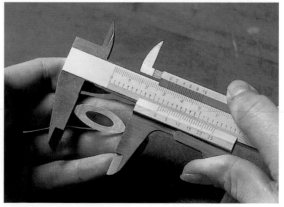

Layers of metal—milled with sheet to texture and thin—are used to make a striking neckpiece.

YOU WILL NEED

- **Basic hand tools (see pages 6-7)**
- **Soldering equipment (see pages 10-11)**
- **Rolling mill**
- **Strip of sheet**
- **Circle of sheet or jump ring (see page 42)**
- **Round wire**

Rolling sheet

1 Anneal, pickle, and rinse a strip of sheet (see pages 34–35).

2 To set the width between rollers on a rolling mill, try pushing the sheet between the rollers. If the sheet passes through the gap, turn the handle on top of the mill until the rollers stop the sheet from passing between them.

3 Support the metal in one hand and turn the handle at the side of the mill so that it draws the sheet through the rollers and releases it on the other side.

4 Check the thickness of the sheet using a vernier caliper. If it is still too thick, repeat steps 2–3 until you achieve the required thickness.

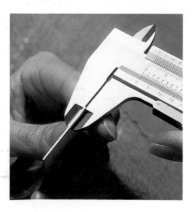

Making ovals

1 Anneal, pickle, and rinse a circle of sheet or a jump ring (see pages 34–35).

2 Follow steps 2–3 of **Rolling sheet** (see left) to set the rollers to the required width and feed the disc or jump ring between the rollers.

3 Check the thickness or length of the metal shape using a vernier caliper. If it is still too thick, repeat step 2 until you achieve the required thickness.

Feed the circle or jump ring through the rollers in the same direction each time, so that it elongates into an oval form.

wire into squares or "D"-sections. The square grooves are useful for shaping and tapering wire. Milling sheet will elongate the piece, for example a circle can be elongated into an oval form; when halving the thickness you will roughly double the length if rolling a sheet in one direction only.

Rolling sheet and wire involves compressing the metal, which means it will work-harden, so remember to anneal frequently and you will not struggle unnecessarily with hardened metal. Overworking the metal will result in split ends and edges.

"D"-shaped wire is inverted to make a pair of simple stone-set gold rings.

Shaping or tapering a wire

The tips of the wires in this neckpiece are milled to add character.

For this technique the rolling mill must have rollers with square grooves.

Forming "D"-shaped wire

For this technique the rolling mill must have "D"-shaped channels on one of the rollers.

1 Anneal, pickle, and rinse a length of round wire (see pages 34–35).

2 Push the wire between the rollers in one of the square grooves. There should be no gap between the rollers, unless the wire is larger than the largest groove.

3 Hold the wire in one hand and turn the handle at the side of the mill so that it draws the wire through the grooved section of the rollers and releases it on the other side. If you want to taper the wire, feed a limited section of it through the rollers, rather than allowing it to pass all the way through.

4 Repeat step 3 as necessary, turning the wire 90° each time, to confirm the shape and prevent an unwanted flange that may appear as metal escapes along the rollers.

1 Anneal, pickle, and rinse a length of round wire (see pages 34–35) .

2 Follow steps 2–3 of **Rolling sheet** (see left) to feed the wire through the "D" shaped section of the rollers.

3 Check the thickness of the shaped wire using a vernier caliper. If it is still too deep in section, repeat step 2 until you achieve the required thickness.

also see the following pages:
Fretwork 26–27 • **Drilling** 32–33
Piercing 22–25 • **Filing** 28–31
Sanding and cleaning up 82–83
Annealing and pickling 34–35
Polishing 84–85

Project 1

Pierced brooch

Piercing sheet metal can leave you with delicate decorative surfaces that are lightweight and practical for jewelry pieces such as brooches and earrings, where weight can, ordinarily, be a problem.

This project shows how the basic piercing and filing techniques can be used to create a piece of jewelry, so you can put the techniques already learned into practice.

YOU WILL NEED

- **Basic hand tools (see pages 6–7)**
- **Soldering equipment (see pages 10–11)**
- **Bangle mandrel**
- **Small mallet**
- **Hand or pendant drill and ¹⁄₃₂ in (1mm) diameter twist drill bit**
- **Planishing hammer**
- **Steel block**
- **Sanding equipment (see page 80)**
- **White spirit**
- **Soft cloth**
- **Polishing equipment (see page 84)**
- **Double-sided adhesive tape**
- **Scissors**
- **Paper**
- **Pencils**
- **Crayon or color pencil**
- **2²⁄₁₆ x 1¾ in (65 x 45mm) strip of ³⁄₆₄ in (1.2mm) thick sheet**
- **6 in (15cm) length of ³⁄₆₄ in (1.5mm) diameter round wire**

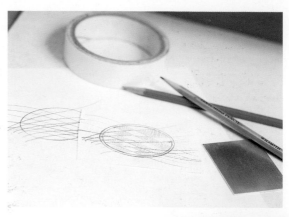

1 Draw an elliptical circle about 2⅜ in (60mm) at the longest point, just smaller than the piece of metal. Draw a second, slightly smaller, elliptical circle inside the first circle to define a border. Draw random diagonal lines crossing each other over the circles.

2 Photocopy the pattern. Color alternate areas between the lines for piercing inside the inner circle. Coloring is a means of defining the pattern for piercing, and limits mistakes when drilling. Cut out the pattern and attach it to a 2²⁄₁₆ x 1¾ in (65 x 45mm) strip of ³⁄₆₄ in (1.2mm) thick sheet using double-sided tape.

3 Drill holes to pass the saw blade through in the colored spaces.

4 Use a piercing saw to pierce the pattern, beginning with the internal spaces, then pierce the outer form.

5 When the piercing is complete, remove the paper pattern. Clean off any stickiness with white spirit on a soft cloth in a well-ventilated area.

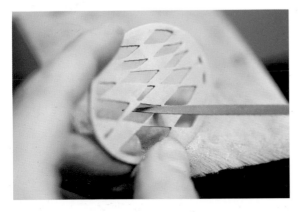

6 Tidy the internal shapes by filing with needle files.

7 Tidy the external form by filing with a hand file.

8 Sand the brooch form using sanding sticks.

9 Anneal, pickle, and rinse the brooch form.

10 Gently curve the brooch by hand over a bangle mandrel, using a small mallet to hammer down any angled areas that remain raised.

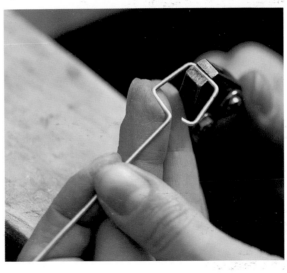

11 Sand any blemishes imparted by hammering using sanding sticks.

12 Polish the brooch using polishing sticks and polishing compounds. Hand polish if possible, since polishing with mops on a pendant drill can cause "drag" marks.

13 Anneal, pickle, and rinse a 6 in (15cm) length of ³⁄₆₄ in (1.5mm) round wire.

14 Form the wire into a square-sided form using parallel pliers. Hold the wire ⁵⁄₁₆ in (5mm) from one end and bend the first corner. Bend the second corner about ⁹⁄₁₆ in (15mm) from the last. Bend the third corner ³⁄₈ in (10mm) from the second corner. Finally, bend the fourth corner ⁹⁄₁₆ in (15mm) from the third.

15 At the point where the straight wire crosses the end of the square-sided form, curve the wire downward to form the pin.

16 Adjust the square so the short end touches the curve of the wire where it drops downward to the pin, as shown above.

17 File the short end to fit the curve of the wire where it drops downward to the pin.

18 File the end of the pin to a taper and a point using a hand file.

19 Form a curve on the pin by hand over the bangle mandrel.

20 Harden the pin by hammering with a planishing hammer on a steel block.

21 Sand and polish the taper and point of the pin.

Forming jump rings

"Jump ring" is the generic term used for simple rings so often used in jewelry. It is important to make uniform jump rings that can be closed with a clean join. This method of making jump rings ensures that each jump ring can be made uniform in shape and size.

The size and function of a jump ring dictates the gauge of wire you use. If it's not going to be soldered, use a heavy-gauge wire that has been hardened. Using two jump rings in conjunction significantly decreases the likelihood that they will come undone.

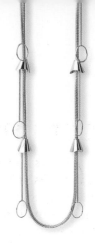

Delicate jump rings are suspended on strands of chain in this necklace.

FORMING JUMP RINGS

YOU WILL NEED

- **Basic hand tools (see pages 6-7)**
- **Round wire ¹⁄₂₅ in (1mm) diameter**
- **Former, such as a metal rod or the shank of a twist drill bit ⅛ in (3mm) in diameter**

1 Hold about 1 in (25 mm) of wire against the bottom of your former and twist the rest of the wire around the former to start a coil.

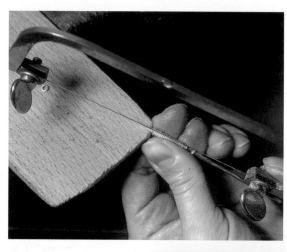

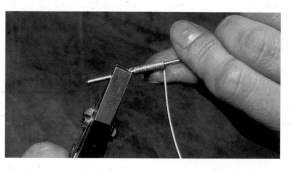

2 It is important to use a downward pressure with your thumb to keep the coil tight. Continue to wrap a close coil around the former until you have as many jump rings as you require. You may want to use parallel pliers or a vise to hold the wire and former.

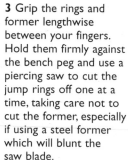

3 Grip the rings and former lengthwise between your fingers. Hold them firmly against the bench peg and use a piercing saw to cut the jump rings off one at a time, taking care not to cut the former, especially if using a steel former which will blunt the saw blade.

4 To open or close a jump ring, hold it in your secondary hand with flat-nosed parallel pliers and use flat-nosed pliers in your primary hand to twist the jump ring open or closed.

Forming ear hooks and hoops

Earring hooks and hoops can be bought, however they are also easily made. Bought hooks can cheapen the overall look of a pair of earrings, but, with a little time spent with wire, pliers, and formers, hooks can be made to look individual—the icing on the cake rather than a functional extra.

You can use any cylindrical form to make hooks and hoops. Make hooks long enough so that they can't easily be pushed out of the ear accidentally. Hoops should be opened and closed by twisting to the side rather than pulling apart, which will deform the shape point.

Freshwater pearls are added as pendants to finish simple hook and hoop earrings.

YOU WILL NEED

- **Basic hand tools (see pages 6-7)**
- **4 x 2 in (50mm) lengths of ½ in (1mm) diameter round wire**
- **⅜ in (10mm) diameter former, such as a metal rod**
- **Steel block**
- **Planishing hammer**
- **¹³⁄₁₆ in (20mm) diameter former, such as a metal rod**

1 Grip the ends of two lengths of round wire with round-nosed pliers and turn them back into small closed loops.

2 Bend the wires by hand around a ⅜ in (10mm) diameter former to make the loop to go through the ear.

Making ear hooks

3 Curve the open wire ends away from the former over a finger to make the hook end.

4 Trim the ends with top cutters if necessary.

5 File (see pages 28–31) the ends to be passed though the ear so there is no sharp point or edge.

6 Hammer the hooks on a steel block using a planishing hammer to flatten and strengthen them.

Making ear hoops

1 Make a coil of wire around a ¾ in (20mm) diameter former by hand.

2 Remove the coil from the former and use round-nosed pliers to turn a closed loop on one end.

3 Use flat-nosed parallel pliers to turn the loop through 90°.

4 Use round-nosed pliers to make a kink at the base of the loop to lower it, so that when the end is cut, it can be secured through it.

5 Cut the hoop off the coil beyond the loop so that the wire can be secured through the loop.

6 Follow steps 5–6 of **Making ear hooks** (see left) to finish. Repeat for second hook.

Forming ring shanks

Rings are one of the most popular forms of jewelry, but they are also one of the most troublesome, due to the size differences of fingers. Whether forming rings from the beginning or altering the size, the process involves moving material with pliers or on a former known as a mandrel or triblet. The width of a ring shank generally affects the size it needs to be to pass over a finger: a wide ring needs to be bigger than a narrow ring to pass over the same knuckle. The vise is integral in this technique as it is used to

In this fanciful ring, the wings are formed from extensions of the ring shank.

FORMING RING SHANKS

YOU WILL NEED

- **Basic hand tools (see pages 6–7)**
- **Soldering equipment (see page 10–11)**
- **Ring mandrel**
- **Bench vise**
- **Large mallet**
- **Small mallet**
- **Ring stick**
- **3⅛ in (80mm) length of ⅛ in (3mm) diameter round wire**
- **3⅛ x ⅜ in (80 x 10mm) strip of ¹⁄₁₆ in (2mm) thick sheet**

Plain, round silver wire formed into a band makes a simple and wearable ring for daily use.

Forming a round-section ring

1 Anneal, pickle, and rinse (see pages 34–35) a length of round wire.

2 Load the handle of a ring mandrel into a bench vise and tighten firmly.

3 Hold the wire over the mandrel so there is an overhang. Ensuring your hand is firmly braced against the mandrel, use a large mallet to hammer firmly down on the wire beyond the point where it touches the mandrel.

4 Feed another roughly ⅝ in (15mm) section of wire through your fingers and repeat step 3. Continue until the curve of wire is at least ¾ of a circle.

5 Load the mandrel, with the ring form still on it, into the vise, making sure you have fiber grips on the vise jaws to protect

the metal. The unbent length of wire should be pointing upward. Using a small mallet, tap the straight length of wire over the mandrel to continue the curve.

6 Holding the mandrel handle, loosen the vise and feed the ring form around so another straight length can be tapped round if necessary. Your wire should now resemble a tight coil.

7 Remove the coil from the mandrel and check the size with a ring stick. If it is too large, place the coil on its side on the bench and tap the side so that it tightens to the size required.

hold both the metal and mandrel, and it can be used to reduce the strength required for forming.

Metal has resilience and will resist your efforts to bend it, so start bending the metal on a smaller diameter than the size of ring you require. Anneal the ring as you form it, and avoid struggling with work-hardened metal.

The most enduring shape for any ring is the fuss-free band so often seen as a wedding band.

A simple shank is topped with a sprung loaded ball-in-column to alter the size of the ring.

Forming a wide ring

8 If it is too small, place it back on the mandrel and tap the face of the ring so it is forced along the mandrel until it is the size required.

9 Cut off the excess wire with a piercing saw (see pages 22–23).

10 Anneal, pickle, and rinse again.

11 Using pliers, close the ring so the two ends meet and flatten it using a mallet on a steel block.

12 Cut through the join, close the ring as in the last step so both ends meet exactly in line. Repeat this step until there is no gap at the join; the ring is then ready for soldering (see pages 62–63).

1 Follow steps 1–4 of **Forming a round-section ring** (see left) using a strip of sheet, until you end up with a "b" shape. Do not hammer on the straight end over the curled end or you will damage the inside of the ring.

2 If the ends are not in line, put the ring into the vise with fiber grips so half of the ring is held with the join just high of the jaws. Tap the side of the ring with a small mallet until it is in line.

3 Follow step 7 of **Forming a round-section ring** (see left) to size the ring, tapping the top of the curled "b" to make it smaller.

4 Use a piercing saw (see pages 22–23) to cut off the straight end of the strip at the point where it meets the curl.

5 Using pliers, close the ring so the ends meet.

6 Flatten the join by hammering with a mallet on the mandrel.

7 Follow step 12 of **Forming a round-section ring** (see left) to finish.

Forming bangles

Bangles are easy to form in comparison to rings because they are much larger in scale, while the metal used to make them is not significantly thicker than that needed to make a ring. This means that they can be partially formed by hand since the material can be readily bent over a mandrel if it is not excessively wide.

Closed bangle forms, like rings, are subject to sizing problems since hands vary considerably in size. Open bangles address this problem, in

Simple silver bangles are an enduring favorite as they are so easy to live with.

Forming a wire bangle

YOU WILL NEED

- **Basic hand tools (see pages 6–7)**
- **Soldering equipment (see pages 10–11)**
- **Large mallet**
- **Small mallet**
- **Steel block**
- **Bangle mandrel**
- **Bench vise with fiber grips**
- **Sandbag**
- **10 in (25cm) length of ⁵⁄₃₂ in (4mm) diameter round wire**

1 Anneal, pickle, and rinse (see pages 34–35) a length of wire.

2 Load a bangle mandrel into a bench vise with fiber grips and tighten it firmly.

3 Hold the wire over the mandrel so there is an overhang. Ensuring your hand is firmly braced against the mandrel, use a large mallet to hammer firmly down on the wire beyond the point where it touches the mandrel.

4 Feed ⁵⁄₈ in (15mm) sections of wire through your fingers and repeat step 3 to continue curving the wire until it forms at least three-quarters of a circle.

5 Hold the curved section of the part-formed bangle firmly against the mandrel with one hand and use the other hand to pull the other end around the mandrel to create a coil.

6 If the bangle is too large, tighten the coiled wire around the mandrel on a narrower point so it tightens to the size required. If it is too small, force it down the mandrel until it reaches the size required, using a mallet if necessary.

7 To correct any undulation in the form, flatten the form by tapping the face with a small mallet on a steel block supported by a sandbag.

8 Cut through the coil with a piercing saw (see pages 22–23). Keep your fingers out of the center of the coil to avoid cutting them.

9 Anneal, pickle, and rinse.

10 Close the bangle by hand and on the mandrel by hammering both ends at the join with a mallet.

11 Cut through the join again and close the bangle so both ends meet exactly in line. Repeat this step until there is no gap (see pages 44–45).

12 Solder the join (see pages 60–61).

13 Hammer the bangle on the mandrel with a mallet, working small sections at a time to ensure the shape is round. Check the reflection inside the bangle: the areas you have hammered will appear polished, unhammered areas will appear matte.

14 Repeat step 7.

some respects, although you need to make sure that the material used to make an open bangle is suitably robust so that the form is not easily distorted.

When making a bangle you will need to consider the distribution of weight if you intend to include any detailing. The heaviest part of the bangle will be inclined to drop below the wrist unless you consider a counterbalance to right the form.

A single wire is used to circumvent the wrist while wire bangles are held in place by a pressed form.

Forming a sheet bangle

YOU WILL NEED

- **Basic hand tools (see pages 6–7)**
- **Soldering equipment (see pages 10–11)**
- **Bangle mandrel**
- **Bench vise with fiber grips**
- **Sandbag**
- **Large mallet**
- **Small mallet**
- **Steel block**
- **10 x ⅜ in (250 x 10mm) strip of ¹⁄₁₆ in (2mm) thick sheet**

1 Follow steps 1–4 of **Forming a wire bangle** (see left) with a strip of sheet.

2 Position the mandrel vertically in the vise. Hold the curved section firmly against the mandrel with one hand and use the other hand to pull the other end around the mandrel to create a "d" shape.

3 Follow step 6 of **Forming a wire bangle** to size the bangle.

4 Follow steps 7–9 of **Forming a wire bangle**, cutting through at the point where the straight piece meets the curl.

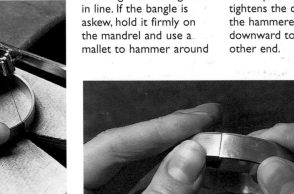

5 Check that the ends of the bangle come together in line. If the bangle is askew, hold it firmly on the mandrel and use a mallet to hammer around the top edge at the end that is pointing up. This tightens the curve so that the hammered end turns downward toward the other end.

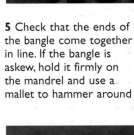

6 Cut through the join again and close the bangle so both ends meet exactly in line. To perfect the join repeat this step until there is no gap.

7 Follow steps 12–13 of **Forming a wire bangle**.

Forging and raising

Forging and raising are techniques for reshaping with controlled force. The choice of hammer face, the support's shape, and the skill of the maker will have a direct effect on the material being manipulated. The principle that needs to be understood is what happens to the metal when it is displaced. A cylindrical hammer (curved in one plane) will displace metal at right angles to the curve, while a spherical hammer will displace material evenly all round.

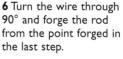

Forging is used with delicacy to create the twisting forms for a lavish organic neckpiece.

FORGING AND RAISING

YOU WILL NEED

- **Basic hand tools (see pages 6–7)**
- **Soldering equipment (see pages 10–11)**
- **Steel block**
- **Raising hammer**
- **Planishing hammer**
- **Blocking hammer**
- **Bench vise with fiber grips**
- **1³⁄₁₆ in (30mm) diameter doming punch**
- **4 in (100mm) length of ⁵⁄₃₂ in (4mm) diameter copper or silver rod or wire**

1 Anneal, pickle, and rinse (see pages 34–35) a length of rod.

2 Hold the end of the rod (about 1in or 2.5cm) on a steel block and stretch the rest by hammering along the length with a raising hammer. Ensure that the hammer blow is square to the steel block: if the hammer is tilted the rod will begin to curl to one side. If you are using the hammer correctly, the blows should be at 90° to the rod and be consecutive, so that there is no unhammered metal between blows. The section should now be rectangular.

3 Turn the rod through 90° and repeat step 2. The section should now be square.

4 Anneal, pickle, and rinse again.

5 Turn the rod through 90° and continue forging. Reduce the forged area by extending the unforged area to begin a taper.

6 Turn the wire through 90° and forge the rod from the point forged in the last step.

7 Repeat steps 4–6, continuing to reduce the area being forged until the rod tapers to a point.

8 Anneal, pickle, and rinse again. Planish—flatten and polish—the tapered rod using a planishing hammer with the work supported on a steel block. Work along the full length of one forged face of the rod; repeat for the other three forged faces.

A flat support doesn't generally alter the shape beyond the effect of the hammer blow; a cylindrical support will increase the directional effect of a cylindrical-faced hammer if used in the same orientation. Raising is a silversmithing technique for "raising" a flat sheet into a curved, open form such as a bowl.

As a means of understanding the effects of a particular hammer or support, modeling clay is a useful trial material. To work the clay, use the hammers and supports as you would for metal; the clay will be displaced like metal but with little effort.

With simple forging and a little raising, a handsome fibula can be created.

9 Anneal, pickle, and rinse again. Spread the unhammered end section by hammering with a raising hammer over a steel block. Begin hammering the end with the hammer face in line with the rod, tilted slightly downward toward the end. With each hammer blow, change the angle of the hammer so that the far end of the hammer face is radiated in an arc form—the end should fan out, thin, and become wedge-shaped in section.

10 Anneal, pickle, and rinse again. Tidy the join between the tapered rod and fanned detail by hammering with a raising hammer.

11 Curve the detail by raising. Position the fan end over a doming punch and hammer with a blocking hammer in a circular action radiating from the center to the edge.

12 Anneal, pickle, and rinse. Clamp the form on the taper just above the detail in a bench vise with fiber grips. Hold the form about 2 in (5cm) above the vise jaws with parallel pliers. Rotate the form to create a twist. Continue until there are as many twists as desired.

Fold forming

The term fold forming is used to describe any form that has a fold in it, although in this case folded sheet is forged to create extravagant three-dimensional, curvaceous, helix forms. There are some useful traits to forged fold-formed pieces, for example, the forms have no solder seams. Despite their volume, forms are generally light as they are usually made of thin sheet; and the natural structures that result from this technique are remarkably strong and flexible. Due to the organic

An undulating fibula is made by fold forming and is detailed with creative texturing.

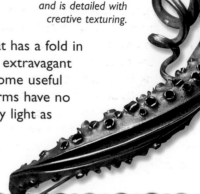

50

YOU WILL NEED

- **Basic hand tools (see pages 6–7)**
- **Soldering equipment (see pages 10–11)**
- **Steel block**
- **Small mallet**
- **Creasing hammer**
- **Bench vise with fiber grips**
- **Blunt knife**
- **4 x 1³⁄₁₆ in (100 x 30mm) strip of ¹⁄₆₄ in (0.4mm) thick sheet**

1 Anneal, pickle, and rinse (see pages 34–35) a strip of sheet.

2 Mark a line down the length of the sheet using dividers set to ⁵⁄₃₂ in (4mm).

3 Place the sheet in a bench vise with fiber grips so the scribed line is level with the top of the jaw of the vise.

4 Bend the sheet at the point of the scribed line by levering it over the vise jaw by hand, then hammering with a mallet to define the fold.

5 Remove the sheet from the vise and complete the fold by bending the sheet by hand.

6 Flatten the fold by hammering with a mallet on a steel block, at either end of the fold first then along it.

7 Anneal and pickle again, rinse and dry thoroughly, as liquid is easily trapped in folds. Mark a line on one side of the fold, ⁵⁄₃₂ in (4mm) from the fold, as shown left, using dividers.

8 Place the folded sheet in the bench vise so the scribed line is level with the fold below the jaw.

9 Pry the folded sheet open using a blunt knife.

10 Lever the two sides of the sheet over the vise jaws by hand, then hammer with a mallet to define the folds.

11 Remove the sheet from the vise and complete the new folds by hand.

12 Anneal and pickle again, rinse and dry thoroughly. Use the mallet over the steel block to hammer the new folds as before.

nature of the process, it is almost impossible to dictate a particular curve or to predict the exact length of a piece: an approximation can be made once you are familiar with the process and its outcomes.

Fold forming is suitable for most metals, from precious metals to steel and aluminum. The thickness of the sheet may need to be varied according to the strength and resilience of the metal to be worked: an original thickness of 1/64 in (0.4mm) works well and this process is best explored using copper.

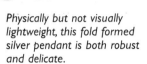

Physically but not visually lightweight, this fold formed silver pendant is both robust and delicate.

13 Using a scriber and steel ruler, mark a tapered line on one side of the folded form, starting the corner at one end to 3/16 in (5mm) from the fold at the other. The effect of the taper is to vary the curve of the form: the narrower the form the tighter the resulting curving helix.

15 Use a hand file to clean and level the edge (see pages 28–31).

17 Anneal and pickle again, rinse thoroughly and dry off. Continue to forge the folded form until the curve is to your satisfaction, remembering to anneal the form before hammering an area that has already been hammered since last annealing.

18 Pry the folds of the form open using a blunt knife to begin opening the form, taking care not to scratch it. Once open slightly, continue to pry the form open by hand to achieve a voluminous helix. If necessary, anneal and pickle again, taking care to rinse and to dry thoroughly.

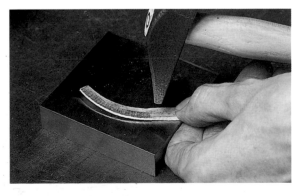

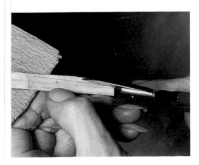

14 Cut along the marked line using tin snips.

16 Forge (see pages 48–49) along the fold of the form, beginning at the narrow end, using a creasing hammer with the work supported on a steel block. Hammer at 90° to the fold with the hammer face level to the work. Ensure the hammer blows are consecutive with no area left unhammered on the fold between blows. The folded sheet should begin to form into a curve.

Soldering simple joints

Soldering is heating two metals with a more fusible alloy, called a "solder," binding them together. Solder joints are more secure if there is a sizable contact area. Silver solder is used to join base metals as well as silver. Gold solders need to be matched for fineness (9, 14, 18, or 22 carat) and color (yellow, white, or red). Solders can be bought in various melting temperatures from easy (low temperature) to hard (high temperature). Platinum needs extremely high temperatures for

A bold silver ring with bar detail soldered on a simple ring shank.

YOU WILL NEED

- **Basic hand tools (see pages 6–7)**
- **Soldering equipment (see pages 10–11)**
- **Hard silver solder**
- **Ring (see pages 40–41)**
- **Very small jump ring**
- **Earring**
- **½ in (0.9 mm) diameter round wire**

Soldering a ring shank

1 Rub a flux cone against the base of a flux dish with a little water until you have a creamy mixture: watery flux is not effective.

2 Using tin snips, fringe the hard solder then cut off "pallions" into a suitable container. The amount of solder required varies according to the size of the join. For a small join like this, two or three ½ in (1mm) square pallions, about ¹⁄₆₄ in (0.5mm) thick should do.

3 On a soldering mat, set up the ring on a soldering block over steel mesh, with the join facing upward.

4 Use a flux brush to paint the prepared flux onto the join.

5 Warm the flux with a soldering torch until it stops bubbling: pallions of solder will be displaced by bubbling flux.

6 Use brass tweezers to place pallions of solder on the join. When positioning, bear in mind that solder is drawn to heat.

soldering. Specialist solders are also available that can withstand the temperatures required for enamelling.

Flux is the generic name for an antioxidant used in the soldering process to abate oxidization caused by heating metal. Flux must be removed by pickling; old flux becomes a barrier once the antioxidant chemicals have been burnt off and is harder than steel, so will damage files and blades. Setting up soldering jobs is the key to success: soldering is easier if the work is supported so it can't move. Use the soldering torch in your secondary hand so your primary hand is free to operate tools. Anneal a "worked" piece before soldering.

Simple hoop earrings where the soldered post is an integral detail.

7 Heat the ring from the back, working the heat forward to the join. Take the piece to temperature swiftly, until it glows bright orange. Once you have reached temperature, soften the flame to stop raising the temperature so quickly, which could melt the piece.

9 Allow the work to cool for a few seconds, then quench in water (see step 4, page 34)

10 Pickle (see steps 5–6, page 35) until all the flux is removed, remembering that flux takes longer to remove than oxide.

11 Rinse the work in cold water.

8 Continue gently heating, taking care to heat the two sides of the join evenly, until the solder becomes molten and flows into the join. Stop heating. If one side becomes hotter than the other the solder is likely to jump to that side as it melts. If this happens, use a solder probe to tease it back across the join.

12 If the join has any gaps, repeat steps 3–11, adding a little more solder if necessary. If the gap is due to the solder not having run completely, you do not need to add more solder, just flux again, and heat the piece for longer.

Soldering an earpost

1 Follow steps 1–8 of **Soldering a ring shank** (see left) to solder a small jump ring to an earring back.

2 Position round wire in the jump ring using sprung tweezers.

3 Follow steps 8–11 of **Soldering a ring shank** (see left).

Bezel stone setting

The bezel, or rub-over, setting consists of a wall of metal that is pushed over a supported stone to stop the stone from dropping out. The height of the bezel—the wall of metal—required for setting is dictated by the proportions of the stone. For a cabochon stone, the top of the setting wall needs to extend up the stone to a point that is smaller in section to that of the base, so that when the wall is pushed over it will hold the stone in. If the wall is too high you will see too much setting and too little stone. For a cut stone, the height of the

A number of stones are bezel-set around the shank of this gold ring.

SOLDERING A HOLLOW FORM

BEZEL STONE SETTING

YOU WILL NEED

- **Basic hand tools (see pages 6–7)**
- **Soldering equipment (see pages 10–11)**
- **Hard solder**
- **Setting equipment (see page 13)**
- **Small mallet**
- **Ring mandrel**
- **Planishing hammer (optional)**
- **Steel block**
- **Coarse sanding paper (see page 80)**
- **Sheet of glass, minimum ³⁄₁₆ in (5mm) thick with sanded edges**
- **Piece of ¹⁄₃₂ in (0.8mm) thick sheet, larger than the formed bezel, for the base plate**
- **Piece of ¹⁄₆₄ in (0.4mm) thick sheet for the bezel**
- **Oval cabochon stone**

1 Establish the height of the bezel using dividers. Place one arm at the base of the stone and set the other to a point over the curve of the stone. Measure the diameter of the stone by wrapping a strip of paper around it, and adding a little extra.

2 Pierce a strip of ¹⁄₆₄ in (0.4mm) sheet (see pages 22–25) to match the measurements taken in step 1.

3 Anneal, pickle, and rinse the strip (see pages 34–35).

4 Wrap the strip around the stone and pierce off the excess sheet.

5 Prepare the join (see pages 44–45).

6 Solder the bezel using hard solder (see pages 60–61).

7 Hammer the bezel circular using a mallet and a ring mandrel (see pages 44–45).

8 Using parallel pliers, squeeze the setting into an oval to fit the stone. If the setting is too small, stretch it by hammering small sections at a time on the ring mandrel with

a planishing hammer. If the setting is too big, cut out a section and repeat steps 5–7.

9 Sand (see pages 80–81) the base of the bezel on a piece of coarse sanding paper supported by a sheet of glass to keep the paper level.

10 Flux the base plate and position the bezel on it, evenly spacing pallions of hard solder around the outside of the bezel. Solder the bezel to the base plate.

wall tends to be less varied as even a large stone has a relatively small dimension between girdle and table. An easy way to estimate the length of metal needed for a setting is to wrap a strip of paper around the stone and add a little extra to account for the thickness of the sheet.

To set a faceted stone or give depth to the setting for a cabochon stone you can create a ledge, or "bearer," on which the stone can rest.

Pearls set in rub-over settings are the center detail in a pair of ornate gold earrings.

Lapis lazuli is set in a rub-over setting to make a simple, pleasing pendant.

11 Pierce out the base plate around the bezel.

12 File (see pages 28–31) and sand the bezel so that you can no longer see the solder seam.

13 Using dividers, mark a ⅛ in (3mm) wide center bar inside the setting. Pierce out the spaces around the bar.

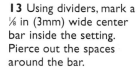

14 File the edges of the bar with a needle file.

15 Prepare a setter's stick by warming setter's wax over a soft flame and building it up on a file handle or other suitable piece of wood. Shape the wax by rolling it, while malleable, on a steel block.

16 Embed the bezel in the warm wax so that the top is exposed, then allow the wax to cool.

17 Position the stone in the setting, holding the setter's stick firmly against the bench peg with your fingers underneath the peg.

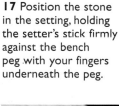

18 Brace your thumbs against the setter's stick, holding a pusher against the top edge of the bezel. Lever your arm upward with a firm, forward pressure to push the bezel over the stone.

19 Repeat on the opposite side of the bezel, then work methodically all the way around the setting until there are no gaps between stone and bezel.

20 Warm the wax over a soft flame and lever the setting out from the softened wax. Remove excess wax with acetone.

Sprues and molds

For all forms of casting, the positioning of the sprue is important, as the sprue is the feed through which the material will flow into a form. If the sprue is too thin, the wax or metal will not flow well; bottlenecks in the form will also cause similar problems. The sprue should be positioned so that the metal flows forward into the piece. It is easier to cut off a sprue if it is sheet-like rather than round in section. Position it considering the flow but also so that it can be

YOU WILL NEED

- **Basic hand tools (see pages 6–7)**
- **Soldering equipment (see pages 10–11)**
- **Hard solder**
- **Sanding equipment (see page 82)**
- **Planishing hammer**
- **Steel block**
- **2 in (50mm) length of ⅛ in (3mm) diameter round wire**
- **Ring for spruing**

1 Anneal, pickle, and rinse (see pages 34–35) a length of wire.

2 Prepare the sprue by using a planishing hammer on the end of the ⅛ in (3mm) sprue wire onto a steel block, splaying the wire into a fan shape.

3 Mark out the profile of the base of the ring on the fanned area of the sprue.

4 Using a piercing saw (see pages 22–25), cut the sprue to match the profile of the ring base by removing the excess material beyond your guideline.

5 Match the curve of the sprue to the curve at the base of the ring by filing with hand files (see pages 28–31).

6 Solder (see pages 62–63) the sprue and ring using hard solder. If you are spruing a piece that has a lot of soldering already, consider using an easy or medium solder to avoid any of your seams and joints running or coming unsoldered. Take care to keep the join clean of surplus solder.

7 Solder again, if necessary, to fill gaps in the seam: a gap can cause an interruption in the flow between sprue and form which could make injecting wax more difficult, and casting less successful.

8 Clean up the join area by filing and sanding (see pages 82–83) if necessary, so that there is no surplus solder on the surface of the form: any blemish that appears on your master will appear on every casting.

9 Present the sprued form to a casting company to make the mold.

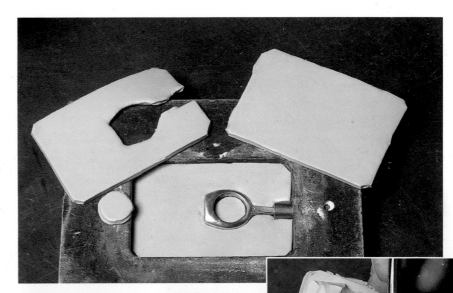

This unusual mold has been made by the meticulous carving of a negative ring form in a pebble.

easily removed by piercing, and so that the area where the sprue was attached can be easily filed up afterward. Spruing work for casting is best done by the maker, although casting companies do sometimes offer this service. The equipment needed for making molds is costly and cutting a mold is a specialist skill; commercial casting companies offer this service. Vulcanized rubber molds require specialist equipment; cold cure molds can be made for masters that are not metal, although this is expensive and not all casting companies offer this service.

The company will sandwich the sprued form between sheets of mold rubber in a metal mold frame. The frame and its contents are then vulcanized: heated and compressed in a press similar to an oversized flower press. The rubber is melted around the form so it fills every crevice. Once the mold has been heated sufficiently the frame is removed from the press and cooled. The rubber mold is then released from the mold frame.

The mold is held in a bench vise and cut open using a brand new blade in a craft hinge to release the metal master inside. Notches are often cut into the top section of the mold so that the two sides of the mold locate: if the mold slips out of alignment a detectable line can appear around the form. Pressurized molten wax can now be injected into the mold to reproduce the form in wax for casting.

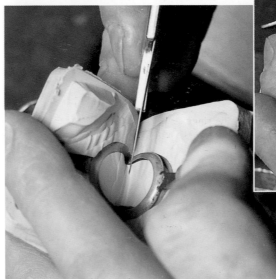

Following intricate forms when cutting the mold takes a good memory and some skill.

also see the following pages:
Carving wax for lost wax casting 72–73
Piercing 22–25 • **Filing** 28–31
Cleaning up castings 74–75
Sanding and cleaning up 82–83
Bezel stone setting 66–67
Annealing and pickling 34–35
Forming a ring shank 44–45
Soldering 62–63 • **Polishing** 84–85

Project 3

Stone-set ring

Wax carving is a relatively rapid and economical technique that can be used in conjunction with other techniques, such as stone setting, to create delicious, individual designs with relative ease.

YOU WILL NEED

- **Basic hand tools (see pages 6–7)**
- **Setting tools (see page 12)**
- **Soldering tools (see page 9)**
- **Hard solder**
- **Sanding equipment (see page 80)**
- **Polishing equipment (see page 82)**
- **Wax ring blank**
- **Wax carving tools (see page 11)**

- **Small mallet**
- **Ring mandrel**
- **Oval stone**
- **Paper**
- **Piece of ¹⁄₆₄ in (0.5mm) thick sheet for the bezel**
- **Piece of ³⁄₆₄ in (1.5mm) thick sheet ¹⁄₁₆ in (2mm) larger all around than the formed bezel, for the base plate**
- **Titanium sheet (optional)**

1 With dividers set to ⅛ in (3mm), mark the width of the ring on a wax ring blank. Use the inner edge of the ring as a guide for the dividers and mark both sides of the wax.

2 Cut away the material beyond the line marked using a piercing saw with a spiral saw blade for wax.

3 Tidy up the profile by filing using a large wax rasp.

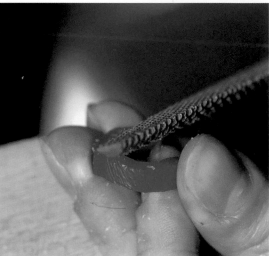

4 Using the round face of the wax rasp, file toward the center of the ring on both edges so the ring has a wavy form, as shown above.

5 File an inverted "V" form down the center of the ring all around the outside using a small wax rasp.

Pa...

Colo...
oxidiz...
eleme...
Oxid...
bloon...
unsuit...
washe...
oxidiz...

di...
fro...
th...
tw...
po...
m...
av...
m...
ba...

Oxi...

YOU V...

- Solde...
  (see
- Prote...
- Safet...
- Paint...
- Bristl...
- Soft...
- Fine...
- Wax
- Oxidi...
  ⅝ in (
  piece
  sulphi...
  (275-...
  and a
  of am...
  Pyrex...
- Dishw...
- Forme...
  and po...
  of jew...

I Wear p...
and safet...
work in a...
area away...

2 Wash t...
with a br...
dishwashi...
warm wat...
degrease.

Pe...

po...

YO

- Pe...
  ca...
  po...
- Bu...
- Tr...
- Re...
- Di...
- Sa...
  pie...
  26...

I P...
load...
trip...
1–2...
har...

6 File with hand and needle files. Clean wax off the files often. Polish using fine wire wool.

7 Present the wax form to a casting company for casting.

8 Pierce off the sprue. Clean up the casting, where necessary, by filing with hand and needle files.

9 Sand the form. As shown left, clean the inside of the ring and the undulations with round-faced sanding sticks or sanding papers in a split pin with a pendant drill. Sand the "V" form with folded sanding papers.

10 Establish the height of the bezel using dividers. Place one arm at the base of the stone and set the other to a point over the curve of the stone. Measure the diameter of the stone by wrapping a strip of paper around it, and add a little extra.

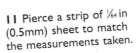

11 Pierce a strip of ¹⁄₆₄ in (0.5mm) sheet to match the measurements taken.

12 Anneal, pickle, and rinse the strip. Prepare the join of the bezel so there is a close join for soldering, then flux and solder using hard solder.

13 Hammer the bezel circular using a small mallet and a ring mandrel.

14 Using parallel pliers, squeeze the setting into an oval to fit your stone and adjust the fit if necessary.

15 Sand the base of the bezel on a piece of coarse sanding paper supported by a sheet of glass.

16 Solder the bezel to the base plate.

17 Using a piercing saw, cut around the bezel leaving a ⁵⁄₃₂ in (4mm) wide tab on a long edge of the stone.

18 Clean the setting by filing and sanding.

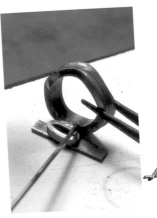

20 Solder the setting, by the curved tab, to the ring. Raise the setting for soldering, if necessary, using titanium sheet.

21 Use a setter's stick and pusher to set the stone in the bezel.

22 Warm the setter's wax over a soft flame and lever the setting out from the softened wax. Remove excess wax with acetone.

23 Finish the ring by polishing.

19 Curve the tab by filing so that it matches a curve on the side of the ring.

Granulation

Granulation has been used as a means of decoration for centuries, and often occurs as dense areas of grains used to create or complement an overall pattern. The grains, or beads, associated with granulation can also be used sparingly to great effect as a means of punctuating a form or surface.

Granulation is used sparingly but decisively in a variety of ways in this series of brooches.

YOU WILL NEED

- **Basic hand tools (see pages 6–7)**
- **Charcoal block**
- **Soldering equipment (see pages 10–11)**
- **Close-meshed plastic strainer**
- **Thin scrap strip of sheet**
- **Round wire ¹⁄₃₂ in (1mm) in diameter**

2 File (see pages 28–31) a rounded end onto a thin strip of sheet and twist it into the surface of a charcoal block to make small indents to house the wire pieces. Position the holes some distance apart: if they are too close the wires may fuse together making larger grains.

3 Place a length of wire over each of the holes in the charcoal block.

1 Prepare wire to be made into granules by cutting it into equal lengths. Using wire cut to a specific length will give you equal sized grains, although you can use scrap sheet if you prefer and sort the grains to size if required afterward.

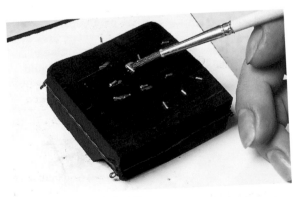

4 Flux each length of wire (see steps 1 and 4, page 60).

5 Use a soldering torch to heat each length of wire until it melts and draws up into a ball, keeping the soldering probe on hand in case the wires move.

6 Allow the grains to cool before pickling (see steps 5–7, page 35). The size of grains makes them difficult to retrieve from pickle, so a close-meshed plastic strainer is a useful pickling aid.

Soldering granulation

Flux the grains and the surface to which the grains are to be soldered and position them on the surface. Then file solder over the grains so that there are tiny bits of solder on and between the grains. Drilling small indents into the surface helps with accurate positioning of the grains for soldering.

Reticulation

Reticulation is metal that is textured by heating until the surface has become molten. On cooling, the surface takes on a random, wrinkled pattern. Sterling silver is best suited to this process, although gold and other materials can be used. Reticulation alters the thickness of sheet because the material's surface is redistributed while molten. This can create areas of resistance noticeable during forming. The overall shape of the sheet is likely to alter so cut out your final design after reticulation to avoid your shape distorting.

Steel that has been subtly textured by reticulation is fashioned into an arresting brooch form.

YOU WILL NEED

- **Soldering equipment (see pages 10–11)**
- **Strip of silver sheet, larger than that needed for the final form**

2 Warm the surface using a soldering torch with a hot, large flame until the flux is glassy, taking it up to temperature—when it glows bright orange —quickly so you do not burn out the flux.

1 Set up a strip of silver sheet on a soldering or charcoal block, and flux the entire surface (see steps 1 and 4, page 62). Make sure you use a creamy flux so that its chemical content is not burnt off before the surface is molten.

3 Continue heating, taking care to watch the surface for signs of it "swimming" as it becomes molten. Soften the flame slightly so that you can control the heat and the sheet does not entirely melt.

4 Tease the molten surface by picking at it or drawing on it with a soldering probe to create peak or wave patterns.

5 When you have achieved the desired surface pattern, allow the piece to cool slightly before quenching, pickling, and rinsing (see pages 34–35).

6 Repeat steps 2–5 if you require a more textured surface.

Engraving

Engraving is the process of making marks on metal by cutting away material using sharp steel tools called gravers. To make precise patterns or formal lettering takes considerable skill and practice, however, most people, with a little time, effort, and patience, can achieve simple patterns and lettering. Try building a selection of sample sheets for practice, and devising textures and patterns that can be applied to your jewelry forms when you feel confident. The marks

This stone-set brooch is lifted out of the ordinary by the exquisite engraving.

YOU WILL NEED

- **Soldering equipment (see pages 10–11)**
- **Small mallet**
- **Polishing equipment (see page 82)**
- **Bench vise with fiber grips**
- **Sandbag**
- **³⁄₃₂ in (2.5mm) square graver**
- **Small mushroom graver handle**
- **Double-sided sharpening stone, coarse (Carborundum) and fine (India)—this must be soaked overnight in machine oil before first used**
- **Arkansas stone**
- **Piece of sheet**
- **Marker pen**
- **Masking tape**
- **Cotton wool**
- **Cloth**
- **Flat-faced block of hard wood**
- **Wintergreen or mineral oil**

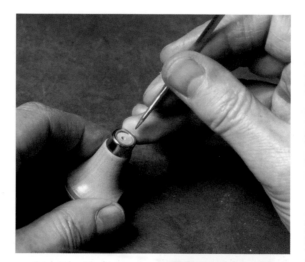

1 Using a soldering torch, heat about ⁹⁄₁₆ in (15mm) of the tang of a ³⁄₃₂ in (2.5mm) square graver to red-hot, then push it into a small mushroom graver handle.

2 Repeat step 1 until the tang is firmly in the handle. About 1 in (25mm) of the tang is burnt into the handle. Place the graver in a bench vise with fiber grips so the tang handle is upward as shown here. Allow the graver to air-cool, then tap the handle with a small mallet to secure it on the tang.

3 Cup the handle in your hand with the graver protruding from between the forefinger and thumb. Using a marker pen, make a mark on the graver about ½–³⁄₈ in (13–10mm) beyond the thumb. The length of the graver including the handle should be about 3½–4 in (90–100mm).

4 Put the graver in the vise so the point marked lies at the lip of the jaw with the tang and handle below the vise. The graver is highly tempered so it is brittle, and excess length can be broken off by a sharp tap with a small mallet. Cover the section to be broken off with a cloth to avoid flying shrapnel.

made by engraving are relatively fine and it is helpful to wear magnifying glasses while working, since this can make a significant difference.

Most shapes of graver should be sharpened to an angle of 30–45°. If the angle is more than 45° it becomes difficult to use because the tip tends to dig into the metal. If the tip becomes too long it may break off. The spitstick and oval graver should be sharpened to an angle of 60–65°.

Even an everyday form can be transformed by carefully engraved highlights.

5 Remove the graver from the vise and, using the coarse (Carborundum) face of a double-sided sharpening stone, grind its cutting face to a 45° angle. Refine it on the finer (India) face.

6 Grind away a section along the upper part of the graver using the coarse face of the sharpening stone. This reduces the area of the face to be polished and allows better visibility of the tool point during engraving. This will leave a rough stoned area, as seen in the picture above.

7 Repeat step 5 to sharpen the cutting face using an Arkansas stone, then grind away a short section of the graver under the cutting face at an angle of about 5°. Take care not to alter the shape of the point and use a drop of oil while grinding.

8 Stab the graver point into a block of hard wood to remove any burs.

9 Prepare the sheet. Metal to be engraved should normally be smooth and flat and have been treated with its final surface finish, i.e. if the piece is to be polished it should be polished before engraving (see pages 84–85).

10 Secure the metal on a block of wood using masking tape that covers about ³⁄₁₆ in (5mm) of the sheet along the entire edge.

11 Hold the graver so your thumb rests on the metal with the work supported on a sandbag, held firmly by the other hand keeping as much of the hand out of the way as possible to limit the chances of injury. Complete control of the graver takes practice; loss of control can result in injury to the hand holding the work.

12 Hold the graver at an angle, placing the point where the cut line should begin. Exert pressure and move the graver forward, away from you, to cut the metal. If the angle is too steep the graver will dig

into the metal and stop cutting, too shallow and it will tend to skip. To lengthen the line cut, use several strokes of the same depth using the graver held at the same angle. A cut should be as long as can be made in one continuous movement. For a curved cut, turn the block toward the graver as you cut forward, using your thumb as a pivot point.

13 To lubricate and prolong tool sharpness, use oil while engraving. Touch the graver tip at intervals in a wad of cotton wool saturated in wintergreen or mineral oil.

Brooch pin, catch, and joint

There are many different ways in which a brooch may be fastened, from an integral fitting on a fibula to a double pin used to fasten a piece that is particularly wide or heavy. Whatever the method used, it should be secure, while allowing the brooch to be easily taken on and off. In a simple, single brooch pin there is generally a hard piece of tapered metal or wire with a pointed end. This is attached to the brooch with a joint that allows the pin to be hinged so that it pivots open and closed. The pin is passed

A tapered silver form becomes an irresistible brooch when a brooch pin is added.

YOU WILL NEED

- **Basic hand tools (see pages 6–7)**
- **Hand or pendant drill and $\frac{1}{32}$ in (1mm) diameter twist drill bit**
- **Pin vise**
- **Soldering equipment (see pages 10–11)**
- **Hard solder**
- **Sanding and polishing equipment (see pages 82–85)**
- **Rivet equipment (see page 112)**
- **Piece of $\frac{3}{64}$ in (2.5 mm) thick sheet, $\frac{1}{4}$ x $\frac{1}{4}$ in (6 x 6mm)**
- **Piece of $2\frac{3}{8}$ x $\frac{3}{8}$ in (60 x 10mm) $\frac{3}{64}$ in (1.5mm) thick sheet**
- **$1\frac{9}{16}$ in (40mm) length of $\frac{3}{64}$ in (1.5mm) diameter round wire**
- **$\frac{1}{32}$ in (1mm) diameter round wire**
- **Brooch form**

Templates

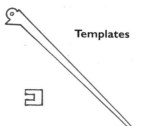

1 Use a scriber and the template (below left) to mark out the brooch pin on $\frac{3}{64}$ in (1.5mm) sheet metal and the joint on $\frac{7}{64}$ in (2.5mm) sheet. The length of the pin is dictated by your form.

2 Pierce out the pin (see pages 22–25).

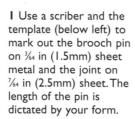

3 File away the sharp edges so that the pin is round in section (see pages 28–31).

4 Hold the pin with parallel pliers, as above, and use needle files to tidy up the wedge-shaped "stop" and the circular part of the joint section of the pin.

5 Use a scriber to mark a point in the center of the circle at the joint section of the pin for drilling.

6 Drill (see pages 32–33) the joint section of the pin at the point marked.

7 Hold the pierced joint with parallel pliers and tidy by filing with needle files.

8 Using dividers, draw a central line down the side of both arms of the joint. Use the dividers to mark a line $\frac{1}{32}$ in (1mm) from the top of the joint.

9 Use the scriber to make an indent where the lines marked in step 8 cross on both arms. Drill, keeping the bit straight so the drilled holes line up when riveted.

though fabric before being secured by a catch. Brooch pins generally have a slight spring action that helps keep the pin in the catch, as a sprung pin has to be depressed to be secured or released.

The open side of the catch should face the base of the brooch, allowing the pin to be secured from the underside so that the weight of the brooch helps hold the pin in the catch. In general the catch is attached on the left side of the form, with the joint on the right, although this favors right-handed people.

The double pin on this brooch form is so alluring it would be a shame to hide it.

10 Make the catch by tapering a length of ³⁄₆₄ in (1.5mm) round wire using a hand file. If you have a pendant drill, hold the wire in the drill and taper it by filing while it is running. If not, hold the wire in a pin vise and file as usual.

11 Using hard solder, solder the catch wire to the back of the brooch (see pages 60–61) about ¾ of the way up the form and about ³⁄₁₆–³⁄₈ in (5–10 mm) from the edge.

12 Position the joint on the back of the brooch so the hole runs vertically, and check that the pin lies horizontal in the joint when secured in the catch. Solder the joint in place.

13 Round off the corners at the top of the joint arms using a needle file.

14 Turn over the catch wire using round-nosed pliers. First turn the end section into a slight curve toward the top of the form, then holding the wire ⅔ of the way down its length, turn it down toward the base of the brooch.

15 Temporarily secure the pin in the joint using a length of ¹⁄₃₂ in (1mm) round wire. Test the stop by trying to secure the pin in the catch. If it lies too high, file the wedge where it touches the joint using a needle file. Keep checking and filing the wedge until the pin can be sprung under the catch.

16 With the catch closed, check the length and trim the pin if it is too long, using top cutters, and file the tip to a point.

17 Sand and polish the pin to make it smooth (see pages 80–83).

18 Countersink the holes of the joint and rivet in the pin using ¹⁄₃₂ in (1mm) round wire (see page 114).

Simple chain

The word "chain" describes a combination of linked repeated forms with flexibility and an indeterminate length. In general, the smaller the links, the more flexible the chain. Many of the chains used today are commercially made with fine wire so that they are more intricate and delicate than could be practicably made by hand.

Plain and formed jump rings are linked to make a simple chain on which to suspend a plethora of pod forms.

Basic round link chain

YOU WILL NEED

- **Basic hand tools (see pages 6–7)**
- **Rolling mill**
- **Soldering equipment (see pages 10–11)**
- **Hard solder**
- **⅛ in (3mm) diameter former**
- **¹⁄₃₂ in (1mm) diameter round wire**

1 Use ¹⁄₃₂ in (1mm) diameter round wire and a ⅛ in (3mm) diameter former to make as many jump rings as you need to form the chain (see page 40).

2 Close one jump ring flat. Flux the join, add a very small pallion of hard solder and solder without pickling afterward (see pages 62–63). Solder is easier to handle for such small joins if it is rolled thin using a rolling mill (see pages 38–39).

3 Wrap another jump ring around the first and close the join.

4 Hold the ring to be soldered with sprung tweezers so that the join is at 12 o'clock. Flux the join and add another very small pallion of thinned hard solder. Solder using a small, fine flame. Present the flame from above the jump ring and lower it until it begins to heat the top jump ring only—the ring directly below must remain unheated to prevent the two rings becoming soldered solid. Again, do not pickle after soldering.

5 Repeat steps 3–4 using as many jump rings as necessary for the length of chain required. Pickle and rinse to finish.

TIP
Use a solder probe to move the solder back into position if it moves as you heat.

Linked oval chain

YOU WILL NEED

- **Basic hand tools (see pages 6–7)**
- **Rolling mill**
- **Soldering equipment (see pages 10–11)**
- **Hard solder**
- **¼ in (6mm) diameter former**
- **¹⁄₁₆ in (2mm) diameter round wire**
- **³⁄₆₄ in (1.5mm) diameter round wire**

1 Use ³⁄₆₄ in (1.5mm) diameter round wire and a ¼ in (6mm) diameter former to make a number of jump rings, dependant on the length of chain you require (see page 40).

2 Use ¹⁄₁₆ in (2mm) diameter round wire and a ¼ in (6mm) diameter former to make the same amount of jump rings again. Close them flat using pliers.